Perspectives on Bullying and Difference

Supporting young people with special
educational needs and/or disabilities in schools

Edited by Colleen McLaughlin,
Richard Byers and Caroline Oliver

NCB's vision is of a society in which children and young people contribute, are valued, and their rights respected. Our mission is to improve children and young people's experiences and life chances, reducing the impact of inequalities. NCB aims to:

- reduce inequalities of opportunity in childhood
- ensure children and young people can use their voice to improve their lives and the lives of those around them
- improve perceptions of children and young people
- enhance the health, learning, experiences and opportunities of children and young people
- encourage the building of positive and supportive relationships for children and young people with families, carers, friends and communities
- provide leadership through the use of evidence and research to improve policy and practice.

NCB has adopted and works within the UN Convention on the Rights of the Child.

Published by the National Children's Bureau

National Children's Bureau, 8 Wakley Street, London EC1V 7QE
Tel: 0207 843 6000
Website: www.ncb.org.uk
Registered charity number: 258825

NCB works in partnership with Children in Scotland (www.childreninscotland.org.uk) and Children in Wales (www.childreninwales.org.uk).

© National Children's Bureau 2012

ISBN: 978 1 907969 36 2

First edition published 2012

British Library Cataloguing in Publication Data
A catalogue record for this book is available from the British Library

Typeset by Saxon Graphics Ltd, Derby, UK
Printed and bound by the Manson Group Ltd, St Albans, UK

Contents

Acknowledgements iv

Introduction 1

1 The research perspective: Vulnerability and prevalence 4

2 The research perspective: Interventions and challenges 21

3 The perspectives of young people with disabilities
   and special educational needs 39

4 The perspectives of parents, carers and families 54

5 The perspective from practitioners and schools 67

6 Looking back and looking forward: Creating an agenda
   for the future 90

References 103

Appendices 113

Glossary 122

Index 123

Acknowledgements

The research that underpins *Perspectives on Bullying and Difference* would not have been possible without the contributions of many individuals and organisations. Most significantly, we acknowledge the support and active participation of colleagues at the Anti-Bullying Alliance and the National Children's Bureau, without whom this work would not have been possible. In addition, we would like to thank Neil Tippett at Goldsmiths, University of London; Jayne Parkin at the National Children's Bureau; Lorraine Petersen at Nasen; and Angela Scott of the Eastern Leadership Centre in Cambridge.

We also wish to thank participants from a number of schools who contributed to the project on which this book is based, including: The Federation of Foxwood and Highview School, Kent; Icknield High School, Beds; Bar Hill Primary School, Cambs; The Wroxham School, Herts; Oak Field School and Sports College, Notts; The Marlborough School and Ormerod Resource Base, Oxon; Bottisham Village College, Cambs; Abbey Meadows Primary School, Cambs; St Philips Primary School, Cambs; Quintin Kynaston School, Greater London; St Andrews C of E Primary School, Cambs; Samuel Whitbread Community College, Beds; The St Christopher School, Essex; and Ventnor Middle School, Isle of Wight.

Colleagues from a range of voluntary organisations, including the Foundation for People with Learning Difficulties, Grapevine, Changing Faces and Mencap, made contributions for which we are grateful. We also owe thanks to the many parents, carers and young people who took time to offer their perspectives.

The editors of this book carried out their work under the aegis of the University of Cambridge Faculty of Education and would like to thank Lyndsay Upex and other colleagues at the Faculty for their support. Colleen McLaughlin is Deputy Head of Faculty and Director of International Initiatives at the Faculty of Education. She has had a life-long interest in bullying, listening to the perspective of the child in education and the personal and social aspects of education, which she has also researched. Richard Byers taught young people with learning difficulties for many years and is now a Lecturer in Special and Inclusive Education at the Faculty of Education. He has research interests in curriculum development and assessment, social and emotional well-being, and participative approaches. Caroline Oliver is a Research Associate who has conducted research at the Faculty over the last 5 years on themes including widening participation and access to Higher Education; the status of teachers and transitions of young people at risk of exclusion.

Introduction

Fergus Crow and Colleen McLaughlin

National Children's Bureau and the University of Cambridge Faculty of Education

It was in 1973 that Dan Olweus' first book, *Aggression in the Schools: Bullies and whipping boys* was first published in Sweden (Olweus 1978 in the UK) and began a tradition of research and development on bullying that has grown in quantity and quality. The work of pioneers such as Olweus in Norway, Smith in the UK, and Rigby in Australia has fundamentally shifted our attitudes and actions in the last 40 years or so. A strong focus has been on children and young people and has involved the development of interventions, policy and research. The notions of 'children's rights' and 'voice' have grown and become widely accepted.

Schools, in particular, exemplify how far we have travelled. We have moved away from a culture of silence about bullying: from a commonly accepted idea that it was not good to 'tell tales'; from notions that little bits of bullying were part of growing up and could be character building. We now accept the notion that we must listen with respect to pupils; and the idea that every child has the right to be safe in and out of school, and that schools should have a whole-school approach, including staff trained to deal with bullying. These are now so firmly established that they are part of the criteria on which schools evaluate themselves and their performance (Ofsted 2011).

Research has developed too, particularly in the years since the publication of major research studies such as that in 1993, which gave the results of Olweus' Bergen intervention; and in 1994, when Smith and Sharp published the results of the Sheffield project. Bullying in schools and other forms of bullying are now internationally on the research agenda. We have learned about the prevalence of bullying; explored definitions; defined different forms of bullying; explored the characteristics of those who bully and those who are bullied; and understood much more about the social dynamics (Smith 2004). Peter Smith has argued that we have not found the 'magic ingredient' of interventions but that:

> *Arguably, the most important factor is the extent to which schools take ownership of the anti-bullying work, whatever form it takes, and push it forward effectively and persistently; this appears to correlate with outcomes more than the extent to which schools receive support from outside.*
>
> (Smith 2004, p.101)

But is this also true of the work on bullying and pupils with special educational needs (SEN) and/or disabilities? This is the question that forms the basis of *Perspectives on Bullying and Difference*.

In the 1990s, Professor Peter Smith and his colleagues first set out the particular distinctiveness of the bullying of children with special educational needs in English schools. Later enshrined in the government's first anti-bullying pack for schools, *Don't Suffer in Silence* (DfES 2000), this work established two principles – ones that the Anti-Bullying Alliance's project, which underpins *Perspectives on Bullying and Difference* a decade later, has confirmed to be as true now as they were then. First, children and young people with SEN and/or disabilities find it harder to report bullying or, as the DfES put it, to 'articulate experiences'. Second, 'they are often at greater risk of being bullied, both directly and indirectly, and usually about their specific difficulties or disability' (DfES 2000, p.16).

The Anti-Bullying Alliance project was set up to further investigate this particular group, to gain a better understanding of the problem and to learn 'what works' in tackling the bullying of children with SEN and/or disabilities. The work was commissioned by the Department for Children, Schools and Families in response to the recommendations of the Lamb Inquiry into special educational needs and/or disabilities and parental confidence in 2009. In the Inquiry, parents identified the bullying of children as a major concern. Not only were parents concerned, there had been disturbing cases of the bullying and harassment of people with disabilities and their carers that had caused the Equality and Human Rights Commission to instigate an inquiry into disability-related harassment.

> *Several serious cases of abuse of disabled people – such as Fiona Pilkington and her daughter, Francecca, who died in 2007 after suffering years of harassment – have been reported in the media over the last few years. Our inquiry shows that harassment of disabled people is a serious problem which needs to be better understood.*
>
> (EHRC 2011, p.3 of Executive Summary)

The Anti-Bullying Alliance formed a project partnership with the University of Cambridge Faculty of Education to consider evidence and research into practice; as well as the Council for Disabled Children and Contact a Family to deliver the children's, and parents' and carers', projects. The incoming government recognised the importance of this work and the project continued, completing in April 2011.

The work comprised a review of existing evidence on the effective approaches to preventing and responding to the bullying of children with SEN and/or disabilities. It also covered questions of whether there was a disproportionate vulnerability to bullying in schools; what was particular about this group of children; and what the challenges in addressing this were for schools. Young people and parents/carers were also asked in a systematic way for their views.

In writing about the young people who are the subject of this book we have adopted, from current UK official usage, the phrase 'special educational needs (SEN) and/or disabilities'. As well as denoting sensory impairments and physical disabilities, this term covers a broad range of conditions. This range includes, for example, autism spectrum disorders (ASD); specific learning difficulties (SpLD) or dyslexia; speech, language and communication needs (SLCN); attention deficit hyperactivity disorder (ADHD); and what are called 'learning difficulties' in educational settings in the UK and known elsewhere as 'learning disabilities' and 'intellectual disabilities'.

Where the context requires it (as, for example, when reporting on research detailing the experiences of particular groups of young people), we repeat more specific terms from the literature. In Chapter 3, which covers the perspectives of young people, we use the phrase 'disabled young people' as it more accurately reflects the respondents who participated in the consultation exercise. We are aware that other forms of terminology ('additional needs', for example, in Scotland or 'exceptionalities' in Canada) are in current use.

Perspectives on Bullying and Difference is concerned with children and young people in primary, secondary and special schools and, unless the context requires the use of the term 'children' to denote younger pupils, we have used the inclusive phrase 'young people' to denote all pupils and students of school age. The phrase 'non-disabled peers' has been used in order to distinguish the majority of school pupils from young people with SEN and/or disabilities.

We define 'bullying' as the repetitive, intentional hurting of one person by another, where the relationship involves an imbalance of power. Bullying can be carried out physically, verbally, emotionally or through cyberspace. This definition does not include random or isolated incidences of aggression or violence, but rather focuses on the kinds of targeted victimisation that is referred to, in other contexts, as harassment or school-based violence.

Perspectives on Bullying and Difference is structured to allow a combination of perspectives on the topic to emerge. Chapters 1 and 2 present the evidence and debates from academic research on the issue. In Chapter 1, the prevalence of this type of bullying is explored, as well as the factors that render this group of young people particularly vulnerable. Chapter 2 considers research on interventions used and the challenges they imply. Chapter 3 is based on the perspectives of young people with SEN and/or disabilities; while Chapter 4 presents parents, carers and families' perspectives. In Chapter 5, we consider a range of current interventions offered in schools to tackle the problem, and consider how far we can accept these practices as 'validated' or proven to be effective. Finally, Chapter 6 offers a review of the evidence in order to draw out the implications for future research and practice development in schools.

The examination of the issue from these different perspectives is one of the features that makes *Perspectives on Bullying and Difference* distinctive and powerful. It enables us to see how the major actors (young people, parents, carers and educational professionals) and those most affected perceive the issues. This we can place alongside the more distanced scrutiny of the research findings on the topic. The synergy is fascinating and the overlap considerable.

1 The research perspective: Vulnerability and prevalence

Richard Byers, Colleen McLaughlin and
Rosie Peppin-Vaughan

University of Cambridge Faculty of Education

This chapter sets out the research evidence concerning the prevalence of bullying and victimisation involving young people with special educational needs (SEN) and/or disabilities, and the factors and conditions that influence these behaviours. It addresses two key questions:

- How vulnerable are young people with SEN and/or disabilities to bullying and victimisation?
- What are the factors that influence the bullying and victimisation of young people with SEN and/or disabilities?

The published research that informs it addresses bullying in both mainstream and specialist settings and tends, most frequently, to focus on the incidence of bullying for young people with specific forms of difficulty or disability. It brings together the findings from this range of often disparate case studies, and draws some more general conclusions about the bullying and victimisation that is experienced by young people with SEN and/or disabilities. The material in Chapters 1 and 2 is based on a comprehensive review of the literature, carried out in partnership between the University of Cambridge Faculty of Education and the Anti-Bullying Alliance (ABA), which was previously published on the ABA website under the title *Responding to Bullying among Children with Special Educational Needs and/or Disabilities* (McLaughlin et al 2010a). Please see Appendix 1 for details of how the literature review was conducted.

How vulnerable are young people with SEN and/or disabilities to bullying and victimisation?

Who is bullied and how much?

The published research reveals that there is a great weight of evidence to confirm that children and young people with SEN and/or disabilities are significantly more likely to be bullied or victimised than their non-disabled peers (see, for example, Salmon and West 2000). This evidence comes from a wide range of settings, for which sample publications are cited, including from: the UK, Thompson et al 1994, and Whitney et al 1994a; Ireland,

O'Moore and Hillery 1989; Scandinavia, Kaukiainen et al 2002, Skär 2003, and Bejerot and Mortberg 2009; the USA, Hemphill and Siperstein 1990, and Twyman et al 2010; Hong Kong, Yuen et al 2007; and Canada, Kuhne and Wiener 2000, Savage 2005, and Luciano and Savage 2007.

The groups of young people in these contexts who are reported to be vulnerable to bullying include those with a wide range of difficulties and impairments, that is, young people:

- with **severe, mild and moderate learning difficulties**, for whom bullying and victimisation are reported by, among others, Gottlieb and Leyser (1981), Taylor et al (1987), Martlew and Hodson (1991), Nabuzoka and Smith (1993), Mishna (2003), Norwich and Kelly (2004) and Twyman et al (2010)
- who experience **speech and language difficulties** (including stammering and difficulties resulting from lip and palate problems) as noted by Mooney and Smith (1995), Hugh-Jones and Smith (1999), Sweeting and West (2001) and Hunt et al (2006)
- with **physical disabilities and impairments**, whose experiences are reported by Yude et al (1998) and Skär (2003)
- who experience difficulties arising from **sensory impairments** (including impairments of hearing and vision) as described by Dixon et al (2004)
- with **autism and autism spectrum disorders** (ASD) for whom Bejerot and Mortberg (2009) and Twyman et al (2010) record difficulties with bullying
- with **attention deficit hyperactivity disorder** (ADHD) and **attention deficit disorder** (ADD) whose experiences are recorded by Twyman et al (2010) and Unnever and Cornell (2003)
- who **achieve higher attainments** (those who are sometimes described as being gifted and talented) whose difficulties are described by Morrison and Furlong (1994) and Peterson and Ray (2006)
- with **specific learning difficulties** (SpLD) or **dyslexia** as noted by Mishna (2003), Savage (2005), Yuen et al (2007) and Ingesson (2007)
- who experience **social, behavioural and emotional difficulties** (SBED) for whom problems with bullying are described by Pope et al (1991) and Johnson et al (2002).

It is reasonable to conclude from this extensive array of evidence that young people with SEN and/or disabilities, who experience a wide spectrum of different difficulties, are affected by bullying. This raises the important question of the severity of this problem and the frequency with which these young people are bullied.

The literature indicates that the rates of vulnerability to bullying for young people with SEN and/or disabilities are very significant. Reports suggest that, for example, bullying may have been experienced by:

- 83 per cent (or roughly eight out of ten) of young people with learning difficulties (see, for example, Luciano and Savage 2007, and Mencap 2007)

- 82 per cent of young people who are disfluent (those with a stammer), 59 per cent of them at least once a week, and 91 per cent by name-calling (Mooney and Smith 1995)
- 70 per cent of children with autistic spectrum disorders combined with other characteristics (for example, obsessive-compulsive disorder (OCD)) (Bejerot and Mortberg 2009)
- 39 per cent of children with speech and language difficulties (Sweeting and West 2001), while Savage (2005) argues that young people with speech difficulties are three times more likely to be bullied than their peers
- 30 per cent of children with reading difficulties (Sweeting and West 2001).

Clearly then, these are not infrequent or insignificant experiences, yet some reports indicate that these problems get worse as young people grow older and move into secondary schools. Mooney and Smith (1995) report that the greatest prevalence of bullying affects those aged 11 to 13. Savage (2005) notes that bullying and isolation get worse as young people with speech difficulties get older; and this is borne out by Martlew and Hodson's results (1991) for young people with learning difficulties. Kuhne and Wiener's research (2000) found that children with learning difficulties were seen by their peers as becoming more dependent and less liked over time, resulting in them being more neglected and rejected as they grew older. This may be related to the generally accepted idea that inclusion for young people with SEN and/or disabilities becomes 'very complex' in the secondary phase of education (European Agency for Development in Special Needs Education 2003), where the effective coordination of responses to individual students and their pastoral needs becomes more challenging.

Some young people experience combinations of difficulties, referred to in the literature as 'comorbid conditions'. A young person with autism, for example, might also have difficulties with OCD; a young person experiencing literacy difficulties (perhaps assessed formally as SpLD) might also experience significant anxiety (or be identified as having ADHD).

The published research suggests that these young people with comorbid conditions are subjected to higher levels of peer victimisation than young people who experience one area of difficulty. Humphrey et al (2007), for example, found that children with ADHD and a comorbid psychiatric condition (particularly a condition with 'externalising features', that is, outward manifestations) were more likely to be victimised by their peers. Bejerot and Mortberg (2009), looking at differences in rates of bullying among children with OCD alone and those with OCD combined with 'autistic traits', found that although both groups were bullied, 70 per cent of the children with comorbid conditions were bullied compared to 50 per cent of the children with OCD alone. In their study, Baumeister et al (2008) found that children with SpLD who also experienced comorbid psychiatric diagnoses reported higher levels of peer victimisation. The research carried out by Montes and Halterman (2007) indicates that children with autism who also had ADHD or ADD experienced a greater risk of being bullied than children with autism alone. Sweeting and West (2001) note that teasing and bullying are additive, meaning that the chances of being bullied are compounded for children with combinations of difficulties or characteristics of 'difference' (see also Sveinsson 2006).

Who tends not to be victimised?

Young people with SEN and/or disabilities are therefore vulnerable to bullying; and young people with combinations of difficulties are even more likely to experience victimisation than young people with a single area of difficulty. However, it seems that there are groups of young people who have individual needs yet do not experience greatly increased rates of bullying. Research reports indicate that young people who have medical conditions alone tend not to be bullied any more than other young people. For example, it appears that young people with cystic fibrosis and young people with 'internalising' mental health problems, such as depression or anxiety, do not report frequent experiences of being bullied or ostracised (Twyman et al 2010). Similarly, Yude and Goodman (1999) report that 'peer problems' for young people with hemiplegia (that is, a condition affecting muscle tone and movement on one side of the body) were not common and could not be predicted either by the visibility of their physical difficulties; their experiences of 'family adversity'; or their apparent 'degree of neurological involvement' (p.7). Sweeting and West (2001) suggest that children who have medical problems (such as asthma or allergies) are, in general, well-liked and accepted by their peers.

What kinds of bullying and victimisation are reported?

Bullying can take a variety of forms. 'Direct', often physical, bullying affects young people in tangible ways but other forms of bullying, including stealing, name-calling or humiliation, can lead to emotional damage. 'Relational' bullying is a form of victimisation in which young people's relationships with their peers are manipulated through ostracism, malicious rumour-mongering or deliberate social exclusion.

Evidence of both direct and relational bullying against children with SEN and/or disabilities can be found in the published research. For example, Mooney and Smith (1995) report that, of the young people with speech difficulties they interviewed, 59 per cent had been physically bullied as children, and 56 per cent had experienced the malicious spreading of rumours. These forms of bullying may be experienced by any young person, although, as has been established, rates of frequency are higher for young people with SEN and/or disabilities. There is also evidence that young people with SEN and/or disabilities may, in some instances, be affected by particular forms of bullying involving ridicule, manipulation and name-calling (this idea is investigated further in Chapter 3, which covers the perspectives of young people). The issue is also raised by Moore (2009); while Mooney and Smith (1995) found that 91 per cent of the young people with speech and language difficulties who were involved in their research had experienced name-calling at school. There are also suggestions (see Sweeting and West 2001, for example) that 'teasing' and 'bullying' are closely related and are experienced by the same young people. Indeed, the Equality and Human Rights Commission (2011, p.111) notes that 'low-level behaviour' has the potential to 'escalate into more extreme behaviour' and that teasing and name-calling, if unchecked, tend to increase in frequency and intensity.

The question of the relationship between 'teasing' and 'name-calling' and more obviously severe and dangerous forms of victimisation is discussed at length in Chapter 3, where the views of young people are presented. However, the literature indicates that pupils with SEN and/or disabilities tend to be 'less accepted and more rejected' by their peers than other young people (Gresham and MacMillan 1997, Nakken and Pijl 2002); and poor acceptance is known to lead to greater risks of victimisation and bullying (Carter and Spencer 2006, de Monchy et al 2004). Frederickson (2010) argues that 'poor social status' within the peer group is one of the key factors leading to increased vulnerability to bullying. Furthermore, Kuhne and Wiener (2000) report that, according to their research, children with learning difficulties were more likely to be socially rejected by their peers. Similarly, the children with physical disabilities in the report by Yude et al (1998) were found to have 'an excess of peer relationship problems' (p.539), despite having been schooled with a stable peer group for more than five years. They were found to be less liked (receiving fewer positive nominations than peers, and more negative ones); be twice as likely to be rejected; have fewer friends; be twice as likely to have no friends; and to be three times more likely to be victimised. They tended not to be bullies themselves. In Twyman et al's work (2010), children with ASD, learning disabilities and ADHD all reported themselves as experiencing 'more clinically significant bullying and/or victimisation experiences' (p.6); while children with ASD reported being both ostracised and victimised.

What is the role of teachers?

A great deal of the research evidence tends to rely on reports of bullying that emanate from young people themselves. Roughly twice as many accounts based on pupil or ex-pupil self-reporting of bullying (or reporting from peers) are published than assessments based on teacher, parent or researcher reports (although some of the pupil self-report data is triangulated against data from adults). Significantly, the research also indicates that teachers are prone to underestimating, undervaluing or discounting reports of bullying from pupils with SEN and/or disabilities.

Researchers consistently suggest that teachers tend to be either unaware of, ignore or underestimate the teasing, bullying and victimisation that affect young people with SEN and/or disabilities (see, for example, Olweus 1978, Besag 1989, Martlew and Hodson 1991). The respondents in Mooney and Smith's (1995) research said that teachers were either unaware of bullying or did nothing about it; and only 20 per cent of teachers were reported to have intervened to help the young people with speech and language difficulties who were being bullied. This is supported by Atlas et al (1998) who argue that '(a) bullying is pervasive in the classroom, (b) teachers are generally unaware of bullying, and (c) the peer group is reluctant to intervene to stop bullying' (p.93). Future discussions focus on the question of why teachers tend not to take the bullying that affects young people with SEN and/or disabilities seriously.

What are the factors that influence the bullying and victimisation of these young people?

What are the characteristics of young people who are bullied or victimised?

Research reports indicate that children with SEN and/or disabilities may have certain characteristics that may make them more vulnerable to bullying. These characteristics include:

- **academic difficulties** and a tendency to perform less well at school (as might be expected, for example, for those with literacy difficulties or learning difficulties) as described by Siperstein and Gottlieb (1977), Olweus (1978), Gottlieb et al (1978), Elam and Sigelman (1983), Whitney et al (1994a and b), Yude and Goodman (1999) and Singer (2005)
- **low self-esteem and anxiety** with tendencies to internalise problems, factors reported by Chazan et al (1994), Dockrell and Lyndsay (2000), Kaukiainen et al (2002) and Moore (2009)
- **differences in physical attributes** (for example, clumsiness, deafness, a visible disability or an impairment) noted in the work of Siperstein and Gottlieb (1977), Henderson and Hall (1982), Besag (1989), Nabuzoka and Smith (1993), Gilmour and Skuse (1996), Stinson et al (1996), King et al (1997), Hurre and Aro (1998), Leff (1999) and Dixon et al (2004)
- **shyness, submissiveness, passivity and an external locus of control** (including being overprotected by parents) described by Olweus (1978) and Moore (2009)
- **uncooperative, disruptive behaviour and aggression** as recorded by Roberts and Zubrick (1992), Erhardt and Hinshaw (1994) and Yude and Goodman (1999)
- **language and communication difficulties**, although the difficulties are more marked for young people with receptive language difficulties and complex language impairments, as noted by Mooney and Smith (1995), Hugh-Jones and Smith (1999), Knox and Conti-Ramsden (2003), Savage (2005) and Luciano and Savage (2007)
- **inappropriate social behaviour** (sometimes referred to in the literature as deficits in social competence) as recorded in work by Gottlieb et al (1978), Siperstein and Bak (1985), Kavale and Forness (1996), Kaukiainen et al (2002), Bauminger et al (2005), and Fox and Boulton (2005)

- **low social status**, a final significant factor noted by Dockrell and Lyndsay (2000).

At this stage, it is important to emphasise that these findings merely indicate a series of correlations between certain characteristics that may be shared by some young people with SEN and/or disabilities who experience bullying, rather than any causal links. Moore (2009) argues that young people with disabilities also seem to be at an increased risk of bullying if they are absent from school more often than their peers (negatively impacting upon their friendships) and if they spend a lot of time with staff (also negatively impacting upon their friendships). Moore also proposes that young people with disabilities may be more vulnerable to bullying if they are less able to defend themselves and less likely to report bullying (for example, if they have fewer friends to support them; if they experience communication difficulties; and if their histories of overprotection by adults mean that they have little experience of standing up for themselves or defending themselves within the peer group). These issues are given further consideration later in this chapter.

Some young people become involved in teasing and bullying others but also get bullied themselves. Nabuzoka and Smith (1993) argue that young people who are aggressive or disruptive are less socially accepted than those who are non-aggressive, and may be bullied because they are seen as 'provocative victims'. They found that young people who were identified by peers as 'being disruptive', 'starting fights', 'seeking help', 'being a bully' and 'being a victim' were more likely to be rejected and 'not liked', and social isolation has been identified as a key factor in increasing vulnerability to bullying. Whitney et al (1992) also suggest that some children with SEN and/or disabilities can be seen as 'provocative victims', becoming involved in teasing and bullying as well as being bullied, because they are less socially competent. Young people with learning disabilities or ADHD may also experience social difficulties – as Holmberg and Hjern (2008), Unnever and Cornell (2003) and Twyman et al (2010) suggest – and risk being regarded as 'provocative victims' by their peers. Social factors seem to be of crucial importance in these instances. Some young people may be unaware that they are causing harm and upset and may misread social cues that prevent 'teasing' becoming more hurtful. Unnever and Cornell (2003) argue that some young people may have difficulty monitoring and controlling their behaviour in social situations. The literature also provides some evidence that children who are rejected by their peers may be likely to respond by adopting bullying behaviours, leading to complex circumstances in which young people emerge as victims as well as being identified as bullies.

How relevant are social skills?

The research reveals that social behaviours are often crucially important factors in instances of peer victimisation, as Frederickson (2010) notes. Bejerot and Mortberg (2009), for example, propose that young people with 'low social ability' are more at risk of being bullied than those with 'high social intelligence'. Nabuzoka and Smith (1993) suggest that low levels of 'competence in handling social situations' (p.1445), together with a lack of knowledge of social rules or 'deficits in decoding social situations' (p.1446), can lead to peer rejection and victimisation among children with learning difficulties. Yude and Goodman (1999) argue that peer group difficulties are often associated with 'constitutional difficulties in social skills and understanding' (p.7). Twyman et al (2010) agree, noting that the prime causative factor that renders children with learning difficulties more likely to be bullied is 'reduced social competence' (p.6). These authors (building on similar points that were made by Kavale and Forness in 1996) argue that young people with learning difficulties may have 'social skills deficits that make it less likely for them to be accepted by their peers or to be chosen as a friend' (p.6) and that these young people may also have 'difficulty in interpreting non-verbal cues, communication messages, and feelings associated with those messages' (p.6).

Twyman et al (2010) propose that children with ADHD tend to be 'less well liked by peers and have fewer friends, because they have difficulty monitoring their behaviour in social situations' (p.6). Law et al (1988) make similar points. In Erhardt and Hinshaw's research (1994), children with ADHD were 'overwhelmingly rejected' by their peers as a result of what were interpreted as their aggressive or non-compliant social behaviours. Yuen et al (2007) report that social adjustment factors (including anger control, compliance with rules, meeting social expectations and interpersonal skills) were found to be significantly associated with bullying among young people with specific learning difficulties (SpLD or dyslexia). Johnson et al (2002) assert that the young people in their research (and boys in particular) were at greatest risk of being bullied when they had poor prosocial skills, difficulties with social interaction, hyperactivity and emotional problems. Frederickson and Furnham (2004) note that low scores on positive social behaviours (for example, being willing to cooperate) can lead to rejection for children with moderate learning difficulties. This remains true even when these young people have moderate negative social behaviour scores (for example, in terms of their tendencies towards aggression), although the research indicates that lower rates of negative behaviour can improve acceptance. Similar findings are noted by Nabozoka and Smith (1993), Roberts and Zubrick (1992) and Taylor et al (1987).

Other work by Kuhne and Wiener (2000) has indicated that children with learning difficulties are less likely to be regarded as cooperative or as leaders than their non-disabled peers, and are therefore more likely to be neglected or rejected. Bejerot and Mortberg (2009) argue that young people with autism are reported to be at particularly high risk of peer victimisation because of their 'deficits in social communication' (p.171); and Little (2002), again, makes similar points. Even young people with 'subtle autistic traits' seem to be at risk: with Bejerot and Mortberg (2009) suggesting that their 'poor social skills rather than social anxiety are intuitively detected by peers, and result in exclusion and bullying' (p.174). Baumeister et al (2008) report that, because children with literacy difficulties, such as SpLD or dyslexia, have 'impaired social tendencies', they tend to have a lower social status than their peers and are therefore more often rejected and victimised. Similar points are made in Kavale and Forness's work (1996).

This significant body of research makes it clear that social skills are of fundamental importance in the bullying and victimisation of young people with SEN and/or disabilities. Much of the language of these reports makes use of the kinds of deficit-focused terminology that seems to locate responsibility for these difficulties with the young people themselves. It will be important to debate whether young people's 'impaired social tendencies', 'reduced social competencies' or 'social deficits' truly give rise to bullying or whether other factors, such as a lack of emphasis on personal, emotional and social issues in the curriculum, may be at fault. The Equality and Human Rights Commission (2011, p.22) notes how authorities tend to focus on the assumed characteristics and vulnerabilities of disabled people, then to restrict their lives, rather than dealing with the problems in the wider context. Parallels may be drawn here with the debates about whether women render themselves vulnerable to sexual violence as a result of the ways in which they dress and behave or whether these crimes arise because of wider and more deep-seated social and interpersonal difficulties. Certainly it is possible to state with confidence that social factors play a major role in bullying. Some authors take this further and argue that language and communication are crucial factors because they provide the means by which social connections are typically established within the peer group. Hemphill and Siperstein (1990), for example, propose that 'because conversation is so often the medium through which children initiate contact, exchange information, and negotiate shared roles, deficits in this particular social area can signal a broader kind of social incompetence' (p.132).

What is the role of language and communication?

In their study, Hemphill and Siperstein (1990) looked at the social aspects of bullying and especially at conversational skills. These authors argue that children who lack these skills may be seen by their peers as 'socially incompetent', adding that children with learning difficulties tend to experience delays in language development, including difficulties in questioning strategies and topic-relevant responding; poor conversation initiation; and trouble maintaining and extending conversations.

As in many other reports, language is seen in the Hemphill and Siperstein study (1990) as having a 'central place' in relation to peer acceptance and social inclusion. The elementary school pupils in their sample 'responded more positively' when the child with mild learning difficulties in the video they watched appeared to have 'competent' conversational skills. These children perceived a peer with mild learning difficulties and poor conversation skills as being socially isolated or 'lonely' – described in the authors' words as being 'on the periphery of classroom social structure' (p.133). This finding applied whether or not the mainstream children knew that the pupils on the video tape had been identified as having learning difficulties, and applied equally to boys and girls. The mainstream children had what the authors describe as good 'discourse awareness' and were effective in detecting strengths and weaknesses in conversation and in identifying specific problems (especially long pauses and lack of active initiation) during conversations.

These results suggest that social competence is defined by linguistic competence. Mooney and Smith (1995) explored this further and found that 84 per cent of the people they interviewed said that they had experienced difficulties, as children who were disfluent, in making friends; explaining that they had not felt that they had 'fitted in' among their peers in school. The authors suggest that speech difficulties mean that young people are less capable of 'asserting and verbally defending themselves' (p.25). Rourke (1989) also notes that poor language skills are a predictor of peer rejection. Savage (2005) argues that children with 'poorer social skills and language difficulties' are more at risk of being bullied than their socially and conversationally more competent peers. This author states that children with 'learning disabilities' in Canada (equivalent to SpLD in the UK) lack 'communicative competence' and have 'reduced empathy', so they become socially rejected and at risk of being bullied. Mishna (2003) reports similar findings.

It may be possible to be more precise about the kinds of language difficulties that lead to peer victimisation. Botting and Conti-Ramsden's research (2000) among children with language impairments indicates that children who experience difficulties only with expressive language (that is, the use of language in order to communicate – for example, by speaking, signing or writing) tend to have fewer social or behavioural problems. These authors report that young people with mixed expressive and receptive difficulties (involving the understanding of language as well as its use) tend to experience more behavioural problems; while those with complex language impairments have more marked social difficulties with their peers because of their 'significant difficulties in understanding the interactions of others' (p.116). There is a great deal of evidence in the published research to indicate that language and communication skills occupy a central role in determining whether or not a young person is bullied.

This point is exemplified in Luciano and Savage's study (2007) in which children with learning difficulties are reported to be more likely to be bullied than their peers. The factors associated by these researchers with an increased risk of bullying include an external locus of control (or the belief that forces outside the self determine outcomes for individuals) and difficulties with receptive language (understanding or comprehension). The authors state that 'this variable plays a key role' (p.27). The children in the study perceived themselves as not being socially accepted, despite the fact that they were being educated in a fully inclusive setting (with no separate teaching) and were not openly 'labelled' as having SEN.

Luciano and Savage go on to maintain that communication problems and 'misinterpretation of social situations' (p.27) may be key elements leading to the increased risk of bullying for young people with SEN and/or disabilities. These authors also argue that internalising problems (such as anxiety and low self-esteem), linked to an external locus of control (expressed as unassertiveness, passivity and submissiveness), mean that children with SEN are 'potential targets for bullies because they are perceived as weak and unlikely to retaliate' (p.27). In a similar way, children with speech and language difficulties are seen as having low self-esteem and as being socially rejected, and thus at risk (Dockrell and Lyndsay 2000).

Being bullied in itself can also lead to further instances of being bullied. Baumeister et al (2008) argue that peer victimisation leads to withdrawal, anxiety, depressive symptoms, social problems, thought problems, attention problems and disruptive behaviour; and that all these symptoms are themselves characteristics that are likely to render young people more likely to be victims of further bullying. Further, these authors propose that children may internalise negative comments from peers and incorporate these into their own negative self-views, becoming, in turn, more depressed and anxious. Given the circular nature of some of these causal factors and their effects, the authors acknowledge that they do not know what comes first – the bullying or the anxiety and depression that lead to more bullying. Storch et al (2003) confirm this ongoing cycle of bullying and social isolation in which rejection by the peer group is closely associated with peer victimisation. As has been suggested above, this rejection seems to be caused most significantly by problems in communication between children with SEN and/or disabilities and their peers and a lack of understanding of social situations. Language and communication are, indeed, central concerns.

What do we know about causal factors?

Although problems in social interactions have sometimes been conceptualised as being caused by 'communication difficulties' located in young people with SEN and/or disabilities, more recent literature presents a different story. It presents the issues as being at least partially the responsibility of schools for failing to promote friendship opportunities; failing to teach social and communication skills; and failing to take responsibility for the 'non-teaching' parts of the school day. Nabuzoka and Smith (1993) suggest that the social difficulties that young people with SEN and/or disabilities experience are particularly significant in 'unstructured situations such as free-play and in the school corridors' (p.1446). These authors argue that young people with learning difficulties may be more able to decode the social context of the classroom, where roles are defined, rules are explicit, and codes of behaviour are reinforced by teachers.

The non-teaching parts of the school day, and the socially unstructured environments outside teaching spaces, have also been reported as generating difficulties for pupils with SEN and/or disabilities in other, more recent, research (see, for example, Byers et al 2008). While much of the literature focuses upon deficits located within young people with SEN and/or disabilities that are assumed to render them liable to be victimised, these authors, and others, emphasise the importance of looking at contextual issues. As Luciano and Savage (2007) note, 'within-child characteristics are modified or even determined by characteristics of the school context in which children operate' (p.17). There is evidence, for example, that the ways in which schooling for pupils with SEN and/or disabilities operates can exacerbate the problems they face by:

- requiring them to be passive and compliant, and failing to teach them to be more assertive
- overprotecting them – a situation also exacerbated by overprotective parents, as noted by Olweus (1978)
- providing them with inappropriate forms of staff support (through the use of learning support assistants (LSAs) for example) and so isolating them from their peer group
- teaching them outside their peer group for all or part of the day – for example, in 'remedial' or 'special' classes (see also Baumeister et al 2008)
- failing to ensure they have equality of physical access to environments and activities, so those with physical disabilities and sensory impairments are unable to participate in activities with their peers
- requiring them to seek help because learning opportunities have not been adjusted in order to be accessible to them – and Sweeting and West (2001) suggest that 'seeking help' is seen by peers as a key characteristic of children with SEN and/or disabilities and as a key reason for their being rejected and victimised.

Contextual features – including staff support, poorly differentiated classroom activity, and separate teaching – may mean that young people with SEN and/or disabilities do not have the right opportunities to forge the social links with their peers that may protect them from bullying. In Nabuzoka and Smith's work (1993), children with learning difficulties were identified by their peers as being 'shy' and as 'seeking help' more often than their peers and therefore as 'not being liked'. Furthermore, the authors found that the children with learning difficulties were being characterised by their peers in terms of their 'vulnerability or inadequacy' (p.1444); and that 'seeking help' was strongly correlated with becoming 'victims of bullying'. Interestingly, Lynas (1986) also notes that the provision of staff support can be seen as reinforcing the characteristic of 'constantly seeking help' in young people with SEN and/or disabilities.

Young people who are not effectively integrated into the flow of classroom activity and who rely on staff support may therefore become victims of increased rates of bullying and teasing. O'Moore and Hillery (1989) found, for example, that children in 'remedial' or 'special' classes experienced twice as much bullying as mainstream pupils. Martlew and Hodson's results (1991) indicate that mainstream students in secondary schools tend to expand their circles of friends as they get older; while young people with moderate learning difficulties report that they are 'subjected to increased amounts of teasing' (p.363) and have fewer friends, both in and out of school. Research reports also indicate that other factors – for example frequent absences from school caused by medical concerns or difficulties in reporting bullying situations because of communication problems (Moore 2009) – can interfere with attempts by young people with SEN and/or disabilities to find ways to 'fit in' with their peer group.

If the key factors in reducing vulnerability to victimisation and bullying are social, then social opportunity is an important issue for schools to consider. As the Equality and Human Rights Commission (2011 p.55) notes, being 'socially isolated' puts people at greater risk of harassment and abuse. The young people interviewed by Skär (2003) felt that their disability 'restricted them in making social relations with their peers' (p.640). They said they felt excluded from their peer group and had few experiences of contact outside school hours. These young people said that, as a result, the attitudes of their peers were negative – and they reported getting teased or taunted with name-calling. The implication is that schools should take more responsibility for promoting access for young people to social situations as well as to educational opportunities.

What do we know about making bullying less likely?

As well as noting that the social fabric of the classroom is an important factor in reducing the likelihood of bullying occurring, research suggests that classrooms with 'cohesion', an emphasis on peer friendships and 'caring' staff attitudes are less likely to have bullying behaviour (Roland and Galloway 2002). Luciano and Savage (2007) argue that, where there are limited opportunities for friendship, there are reduced opportunities to learn social skills – and that the risk of bullying is therefore increased. In earlier research, Savage (2005) found that, while children with speech and language difficulties do report three times more bullying than their mainstream peers, this varies according to which class they are in. Savage's findings suggest that these children are not necessarily more prone to bullying than their peers but that their experiences depend, to some extent, on where they are taught. Classrooms in which children are encouraged to be willing to play and 'hang out with' (that is, not 'work with' and not necessarily 'be best friends with') children with speech and language difficulties are reported by Savage (2005) to be less likely to have bullying. Frederickson and Furnham (2004) found similar results for pupils with moderate learning difficulties. This suggests that peer acceptance (particularly in non-classroom and playground settings) by large numbers of peers (numerous 'bystanders' rather than a few good friends) is a 'protective factor'. Rather than regarding social isolation as occurring as the result of deficits in young people with SEN and/or disabilities, the facilitation of peer acceptance should arguably be seen as one of the professional responsibilities of school staff.

The research suggests that peer acceptance is a protective factor in relation to victimisation; and that peer rejection increases the likelihood of young people being victimised (Perry et al 1988). Moore (2009) suggests that the factors that help to protect young people from bullying and victimisation include secure friendships, which can bolster self-esteem and offer direct support to vulnerable young people; self-confidence; and peer acceptance, which can be enhanced through 'buddying' and peer support arrangements, although Moore notes that the evidence for the efficacy of these is 'mixed'. Nabuzoka and Smith's work (1993) indicates that being seen as 'cooperative' is a protective factor (their research suggests that this is true even where pupils with learning difficulties are also seen as being 'shy' and 'seeking help'). Bejerot and Mortberg (2009) suggest that social anxiety coupled with good social skills may also provide some protection against peer victimisation.

Whitney et al (1992) argue that young people with SEN and/or disabilities are more likely to be bullied because they tend to have fewer friends and therefore lack the protection that a peer group can offer. Luciano and Savage (2007) argue that students with SEN may not form friendships that can protect them against being bullied. This idea is also put forward in a series of other publications, including papers by: Hugh-Jones and Smith (1999), Chazan et al (1994), Coie and Cillessen (1993), Geisthardt and Munsch (1996), Nabuzoka and Smith (1993), Rigby (2000), Roberts and Zubrick (1992), Savage (2005), Wenz-Gross and Siperstein (1997) and Whitney et al (1994a and b). This is clearly an important proposition. Furthermore, peer rejection, according to Luciano and Savage (2007), is associated with peer victimisation. These authors suggest that there is some evidence that attending inclusive schools can help by providing opportunities for peer group association and therefore social support. Savage (2005) notes that the most effective factor protecting young people against bullying and victimisation is acknowledged to be the social support provided by friendships or even acquaintances with peers.

However, Cavallaro and Porter (1980), Guralnick (1986) and Martlew and Cooksey (1989) all note that pupils with mild or moderate learning difficulties interact less with their peers in integrated settings than do other pupils. Interactions for pupils with severe learning difficulties are reported to be 'minimal' (Guralnick 1986). Luciano and Savage (2007) concede that there is also evidence that young people with SEN and/or disabilities are bullied more often in mainstream settings. They suggest that inclusive settings (and even schools with 'thoughtful anti-bullying policies', p.27) do not, in themselves, confer protection. Young people with SEN and/or disabilities may still have 'low social status' (Luciano and Savage 2007, p.26), have few friends, and be socially rejected.

It is clear, then, that schools have a responsibility to focus on social issues; to teach social and communication skills; and to foster the kinds of social interactions between young people with SEN and/or disabilities and their mainstream peers that will make bullying less likely to happen or to be tolerated. There is also some evidence that actively teaching disability awareness and helping young people to understand and empathise with their peers with SEN and/or disabilities can be productive. For example, Law et al (1988) suggest that the behaviours of pupils with ADHD are likely to lead to rejection by peers. But Frederickson (2010) argues that providing relevant information and 'clearly acknowledging differences' to classmates, using a sensitive process of identification and 'labelling', can have 'protective' effects (see also Bromfield et al 1986) and enhance inclusion. The Equality and Human Rights Commission (2011, p.165) also notes the need to 'change attitudes' towards disabled people and calls for 'improved awareness-raising activities'.

This position is supported by evidence (Newberry and Parish 1987) that indicates that peers tend to be more accepting of, and to make 'allowances' for, children with more 'visible' disabilities (for example, physical disabilities, visual impairments and hearing impairments). There is also some evidence that children with 'less severe special needs' in mainstream education (that is, children with mild or 'hidden' difficulties) experience greater levels of rejection than 'former special school pupils' (Lewis and Lewis 1988, Sale and Carey 1995); and that they are more likely themselves to engage in bullying behaviour (Frederickson et al 2007). The process of making 'special', 'additional' and 'individual' needs more explicit is controversial. Practice seems to have moved away from attempts to build empathy in the peer group through awareness-raising and the explication of difficulties and disabilities. However, the evidence seems to suggest that schools should look again at these possibilities.

What conclusions about prevalence can be drawn from the research?

There is a great weight of evidence that confirms that young people with SEN and/or disabilities are significantly more likely to be bullied or victimised than their non-disabled peers. Further, the rates of vulnerability to bullying for young people with SEN and/or disabilities are very significant. Reports also suggest that teachers tend to underestimate, undervalue or discount reports of bullying from pupils with SEN and/or disabilities.

Pupils with SEN and/or disabilities tend to be less accepted and more rejected by their peers than other children, even when they have studied within a stable peer group for a number of years. Poor peer acceptance is known to lead to greater risk of victimisation and bullying. Some reports indicate that these problems get worse as young people grow older and move into secondary schools. Further, children with comorbid conditions or combinations of difficulties report higher levels of peer victimisation. Teasing and bullying are reported to be additive, meaning that the chances of being bullied are compounded for children with combinations of difficulties or characteristics of 'difference'.

The research implies that young people with SEN and/or disabilities have many characteristics that make them vulnerable to bullying, including lower academic attainment; physical differences; shyness and passivity; low self-esteem and anxiety; and behaviour that challenges other people. Being bullied, in itself, seems likely to lead to further bullying. Some young people with SEN and/or disabilities (often those with learning disabilities or ADHD) can be seen as 'provocative victims', becoming involved in teasing and bullying as well as being bullied themselves, arguably because they have difficulty monitoring and controlling their behaviour in social situations. There is also some evidence that young people who are rejected may be more likely to respond by adopting bullying behaviours. However, the research strongly suggests that the key determinants of vulnerability to bullying are associated with language and communication, social skills, and status.

Social behaviours are crucially important with regard to peer victimisation. Young people with SEN and/or disabilities are often described in the research as being at risk of being bullied because of their 'low social ability', 'deficits in decoding social situations', 'reduced social competence', or 'impaired social tendencies'. There is wide agreement that social issues relating to peer rejection are key factors in the bullying of young people with SEN and/or disabilities. Some authors, however, also acknowledge the significance of language and communication issues and the difficulties that some young people may experience in interpreting non-verbal cues, communication messages, and the feelings associated with those messages.

The research suggests that language and communication have central places in the bullying and victimisation of young people with SEN and/or disabilities – because dialogue is generally the medium through which young people initiate contact, exchange information and negotiate shared roles, and because young people with SEN and/or disabilities frequently experience delays in language development. Non-disabled young people in the mainstream of education tend to have good 'discourse awareness' and to be good at detecting strengths and weaknesses in conversation. They may define social competence in terms of linguistic competence and respond accordingly, so that poor language skills (and particularly poor receptive language skills) become a predictor of peer rejection.

Communication problems and the misinterpretation of social situations may be key elements leading to an increased risk of bullying for young people with SEN and/or disabilities. Social isolation and victimisation can lead to further exacerbated victimisation in an ongoing cycle of bullying and rejection.

Aspects of service design and provision, and the strategies adopted by professionals, can also render young people more liable to be bullied. The research indicates that isolation and victimisation are at least partially the responsibility of schools for failing to promote friendship opportunities; failing to teach social skills; and failing to take responsibility for the 'non-teaching' parts of the school day. The difficulties that young people with SEN and/or disabilities experience are particularly significant in unstructured situations, such as during free-play and in school corridors.

There is also evidence that the ways in which schooling for pupils with SEN and/or disabilities operates can exacerbate the problems that young people face, by requiring them to be passive and compliant; over-protecting them; providing them with inappropriate staff support; teaching them outside their peer group; failing to ensure equality of physical access to environments and activities; and requiring them to seek help because the work has not been adjusted so as to be accessible to them. Contextual features – including staff support, poorly differentiated teaching and separate teaching – may mean that young people with SEN and/or disabilities do not have the right opportunities to forge protective links with their peers. Young people who are not effectively integrated and who rely on staff support may become victims of bullying and teasing.

Managing the relationships between whole-school practices and young people's special or additional needs, and the support that may be provided in order to meet them, is a key issue for schools. The next chapter therefore goes on to review the messages that the research can provide on interventions.

2 The research perspective: Interventions and challenges

Richard Byers, Colleen McLaughlin and
Rosie Peppin-Vaughan

University of Cambridge Faculty of Education

This chapter sets out the research evidence concerning the responses that schools make to the challenges raised by the bullying and victimisation of young people with SEN and/or disabilities. It addresses two key questions:

- What are reported to be the most effective approaches that schools can take to prevent and respond to the bullying that affects young people with SEN and/or disabilities?
- What are the challenges that schools face in effectively preventing and responding to this bullying?

The chapter begins with an examination of the general state of the research on interventions and goes on to review the methodological and philosophical issues that arise. It explores the research studies focusing on prevention and response, and discusses the agenda for future research and practice. It ends with a summary of the conclusions that can be drawn from the research and the main messages to be taken forward into further developments.

What are reported to be the most effective approaches that schools can take to prevent and respond to this bullying?

What kinds of research have focused on interventions?

Research on the topic of bullying interventions has developed considerably over the last 15 years. The particular focus on interventions for pupils with SEN and/or disabilities began with studies such as those by Thompson et al (1994) based in Sheffield. Since then, there has been greater research activity and many reviews of research internationally (see, for example, Farmer 1993, Gresham and MacMillan 1997, Kavale and Forness 1996, Frederickson et al 2007, and Frederickson 2010). These reviews of research clearly highlight the finding that many students with SEN and/or disabilities encounter social difficulties in school and are not well accepted by their peers. The consequences of experiences like these have been extensively studied in students who do not have additional needs. Farmer (1993), Kamps and Tankersley (1996) and Kauffman (1999), among others, indicate that peer rejection and social skill deficits are often associated with later adjustment problems.

The research that examines bullying as it affects young people with SEN and/or disabilities includes a mix of detailed qualitative studies focused on practice (including accounts by psychologists, advisory teachers, classroom teachers and support staff), together with substantial reviews of prior research and fresh inquiries carried out by university-based researchers. There is also a useful literature that examines the views of young people themselves, which is largely found in accounts by non-governmental organisations or specialist advocacy groups. The focus of these studies has been largely on peer relations and how they can be developed.

Guidance on dealing with bullying in schools promotes the process of accessing students' views (DCSF 2008a); and this is also raised by others (Hodson et al 2005). A Mencap study (2007) highlights this as an important methodological issue. Guidance on the centrality of the student voice raises the issue of how school staff access the experiences of young people with SEN and/or disabilities in relation to bullying in ways that are economical of effort and pragmatic in school situations. Marini et al (2001) write about the importance of this activity, arguing that staff need to assess the bullying of young people with SEN and/or disabilities in schools accurately, especially since the tendency to underestimate it has been demonstrated. Byers et al (2008) provide one example of school-based participatory research that highlights and tackles the issues of bullying and social isolation for young people with SEN and/or disabilities in mainstream schools. Lewis and Lindsay (2000) and Porter and Lacey (2005) provide important guidance on conducting research and consultation processes that effectively include young people with SEN and/or disabilities.

Many writers, including Frederickson (2010), Rose and Howley (2003) and Watts and Erevelles (2004), draw our attention to matters of conceptualisation and its impact on intervention. They show that the ways in which staff conceptualise bullying (or school violence, in an alternative terminology) and disability can lead to notions of blame and responsibility and thus dictate the locus of intervention. If staff locate problems within students (whether bullies or victims), then their responses to bullying will involve intervening in this domain and focusing on individuals. Their attempts will be to target and somehow to change either the perpetrator or those who are bullied. The significant movement in the literature, however, has been towards an acceptance of the need to conceptualise bullying as located within the social context of schools and young people's lives. As a result the focus, in both preventing and responding to bullying for young people with SEN and/or disabilities, shifts away from the individual and onto interactions between peers and peer relations.

According to Greenham (1999), this shift in the research from a concentration on the individual cognitive or behavioural aspects of the problem to the psychosocial domain, with a particular focus on peer relations, has highlighted the difficulties of social competence, social cognition, peer status and peer acceptance that affect some young people. There have been many research studies that have focused upon the inclusion of young people with SEN and/or disabilities in mainstream settings; and researchers (including

Whitney et al 1992, Farmer 1993, Greenham 1999, Marini et al 2001, Mishna 2003, and Frederickson et al 2007) have studied the different elements of peer relations. When the young people with physical disabilities that Skär (2003) interviewed were teased, taunted or called names, for example, they felt they could respond either by becoming a joker and using the abusive terms themselves – or by avoiding contact with peers. These young people sought friendships outside their age group (with both younger and older friends) and outside their gender (disabled boys found girls to be 'kinder'). They also liked socialising on the internet, where they did not have to reveal their disability. However, Didden et al (2009) show that cyberbullying is very prominent among young people who may withdraw as a result of their disability and depend heavily on the internet for social engagement. As a consequence, this form of victimisation frequently affects young people with SEN and/or disabilities. These young people are more vulnerable to cyberbullying since they spend more time using digital forms of communication.

It is clear that there is a strong case for intervening both preventatively and reactively. A powerful case can also be made for carefully monitoring the bullying of pupils with SEN and/or disabilities, since bullying and victimisation affecting this group of young people have been shown by a series of authors – including Pepler et al (1994), Sharp (1996), Hanish and Guerra (2000) and Frederickson et al (2007) – to be significantly underestimated.

What does the research say about preventative interventions?

Much of the research and subsequent discussion has centred upon the social consequences for young people with SEN and/or disabilities of being included in mainstream settings. These studies are important because they have much to reveal about the social interactions and social rejection that are so central to bullying. Frederickson (2010) concludes that reviews comparing inclusive settings with separate special schools or classes, such as those by Baker et al (1994–5) or Lindsay (2007), have reported small positive benefits for inclusion. However, reviews comparing social outcomes for young people within inclusive settings, such as those by Gresham and MacMillan (1997) and Nakken and Pijl (2002), have found that pupils with SEN and/or disabilities are generally less accepted and more rejected than their non-disabled peers. The research also shows that planned preventative interventions make a difference and improve matters; and that if there is no intervention then bullying can be worse in mainstream settings. Rose et al (2009) suggest that inclusive settings may lead to lower levels of bullying for children with SEN and/or disabilities because they may allow these young people to develop social skills, through behavioural modelling, and to generally enhance acceptance and participation. In contrast, Martlew and Hodson (1991) argue that inclusion may maintain or exacerbate victimisation if students are not fully integrated into peer groups. Mishna (2003) adds that this isolation then further limits opportunities for young people to learn, practise, and receive validation for social skills; while Rose et al (2009 p.764) note that ineffective integrative practices may also 'hinder the ability to develop a protective peer base'. It is apparent, therefore, that there is a need for planned interventions. These interventions also need to be carefully targeted, and to be sophisticated in their responses to particular socially contextualised needs and to the different challenges presented by particular disabilities.

Farmer (1993) summarises how research in the 1980s and '90s focused on social skills training and peer support strategies. Yude and Goodman (1999), for example, suggest treating 'externalising problems' with behaviour management or medication, or by helping children to develop better social skills and understandings. Yude et al (1998 p.540) recommend (speculatively) a 'whole-school approach that fosters inclusive attitudes and increases disability awareness'; 'coaching in social skills'; and 'training in mentalising techniques'. These strategies were found to be useful but the outcomes were modest because they did not take into account the social context or the contextual factors that maintain the aggressive behaviour, which is often related to peer status and role. The effectiveness of individual and peer-support interventions depends, in part, on whether they are supported by the general classroom and school social climate.

> *While assisting aggressive students to develop stronger social competencies and friendships, educators must also be aware of the ways in which the social context can support problem behaviour and should develop strategies to inhibit the emergence of interchanges that maintain antisocial behaviour. This does not mean ignoring the focus on peer rejection and social skills training. Rather, the framework of interventions should be broadened to include a more direct focus on social structures, including students' peer affiliations and social roles in the classroom and school, and providing students with opportunities to develop positive roles and associations outside the instructional setting.*
>
> (Farmer 1993, p.206)

Mishna (2003) has shown the need for adult support: both to prepare the group proactively in order to prevent rejection or victimisation, and to help the group accept a young person who has already been victimised. Adults are also essential to changing the social contexts of, and interactions within, the school and the classroom. Dixon (2006), in a study of bullying affecting deaf or hearing impaired young people, argues that not enough attention is given to helping adults to work with the emotional aspects of bullying as it affects pupils with SEN and/or disabilities. Dixon investigated teachers' use of a framework of interventions that targeted emotional change, cognitive change and behavioural change. She found that most of the interventions adopted by teachers were in the cognitive category. While the model of emotional, cognitive and behavioural change provides a useful overall framework for shaping interventions in general, most of the work reported in the literature focuses on changing the nature of peer interactions or on using the peer group as a support.

In what ways are peers reported to be involved in interventions?

The work of Young (1998), Greenham (1999), Etherington (2007) and Frederickson (2010) indicates that peer interventions tend to fall into two main categories: those that promote direct peer support; and those that aim to engage the empathy of peers through peer education, then to harness that empathy in support of students with SEN and/or disabilities. Frederickson (2010) argues that the risks associated with the 'labelling' of these young people have been overstated. Instead, she proposes that there is evidence that including the peer group in open communication about additional needs and preferred responses to these needs provides, in many cases, an important foundation for building positive classroom relationships. Peer education aims to provide information by a range of means and with due consideration to the context. Frederickson (2010 p.8), citing Campbell (2006), argues that communicating ideas about SEN and/or disability to the peer group must take account of 'four components of persuasive communication'. Campbell refers to these components as: the source ('who'), the message ('what'), the channel or medium ('how') and the receiver or target audience ('to whom'); and argues that these components should all be investigated when developing the knowledge base about how best to present initial information concerning SEN and/or disability to classmates. Campbell (2007) also argues that it is important to provide explanatory information in addition to descriptive information.

The strategies used to educate peers may involve using a variety of presentational devices in order to inform pupils about specific aspects of SEN and/or disability. Hunt et al (1996) and Turnbull (2006) describe using multimedia presentations, along with active learning tasks, in classes which already included, or were about to include, a young person with SEN and/or disabilities. These presentations informed the classmates about the difficulties experienced by particular young people and the nature of their individual needs. This seemed to signal to peers that 'these pupils are deserving of special attention' (Frederickson 2010, p.6). These studies provide evidence of the effectiveness of peer education interventions in increasing positive interactions between the young people with SEN and/or disabilities and their peers, and in securing improved levels of acceptance. The activation of empathy and understanding for pupils with SEN and/or disabilities is seen as the mechanism operating here. Frederickson (2010) argues that non-disabled peers gain rewards, including feelings of higher self-esteem, from helping classmates who experience difficulties. A strong argument is made in these studies for the positive value of raising awareness of disability, but there is also a need to harness more active forms of peer support and to intervene in the social context.

Saylor and Leach (2009, pp.79–80) describe the Peer EXPRESS (Experiences to Promote Recreation, Exposure, and Social Skills) programme, 'whose mission was to bring peers with and without disabilities together for shared arts, sports, camps, service, and leisure activities in school and in the community'. The authors conclude that the programme resulted in increased empathy and ability to relate, and in a significant decrease in bullying behaviour. Other strategies that are reported in the literature and that engage peers directly in support roles include buddy systems (Frederickson 2010); Circles of Friends (Etherington 2007); and peer mediation (Warne 2003). Moore (2009) recommends helping to foster friendships, peer support or 'buddying', in addition to involving young people with SEN and/or disabilities in developing a school policy on bullying. A body of evidence is building for the strength and efficacy of peer education and peer support initiatives, but this research field is in its early stages and the need to evaluate programmes rigorously and over time remains.

What interventions do practitioners use?

A number of authors emphasise that direct teaching to support language and communication skills among pupils with SEN and/or disabilities can be effective in reducing levels of isolation, victimisation and bullying. Hemphill and Siperstein (1990), for example, speculate that focused work on language skills for pupils with moderate learning difficulties might enhance their social acceptance and inclusion. Goldman (1987) proposes that support for young people with language needs should focus on social aspects; and Vetter (1982) argues that teachers should be better equipped to differentiate their interventions according to the precise area of language need. The work carried out by Botting and Conti-Ramsden (2000) indicates that support should focus particularly on receptive language skills and social understanding.

Other interventions that have been found to be useful in the classroom relate directly to interactions occurring within teaching and learning activities and involve teaching young people how to interact more effectively in groups and within the learning context. These interventions also involve teachers in structuring learning tasks so that they necessarily involve genuine collaboration and interaction. Rose and Howley (2003), for example, report using a form of group work they refer to as 'jigsawing' within the structured and differentiated teaching they investigated. Mishna (2003) has also argued that social education must include the development of community awareness about bullying and the particular vulnerability of young people with SEN and/or disabilities.

Some action that is recommended in relation to reducing bullying and victimisation focuses on the wider peer group. Woods and White (2005), for example, identify two kinds of bullying behaviour: 'direct bullying' (such as hitting, kicking or taking belongings) and 'relational bullying' (which is more common and causes harm through the manipulation of social relations by name-calling, spreading rumours and social exclusion). The authors then identify four kinds of children: 'pure bullies'; 'pure victims'; 'bully-victims'; and 'neutral' (bystanders or defenders of the victim). They propose that children with a bully-victim profile who are involved in direct and relational bullying experience the highest levels of arousal (for example, feeling both anxious and provocative); they note that victim status (involving shy, anxious and avoidant mental states) and behaviour problems are also associated with high levels of arousal. The children with the lowest levels of arousal (those who are 'cool' – but seeking stimulation) tend to be direct 'pure' bullies. The authors go on to propose that schools need to understand and manage the links between arousal levels and pupil behaviour. They argue that school strategies designed to reduce arousal levels (including calm environments; the presence of authority figures; use of relaxation techniques; use of self-talk techniques; the direct teaching of problem solving; and teaching children to cope with failure) can reduce bullying. These authors also suggest that schools can work to raise arousal levels and reduce aggression (for example, for potential direct bullies) by offering alternative forms of excitement and challenge (for example, through sports activity).

Other studies have focused upon the particular needs of pupils, for example, those with Tourette syndrome (Murphy and Heyman 2007); those who are deaf (Dixon 2006); those with Asperger's syndrome (Attwood 2004); and those who stammer (Turnbull 2006). These authors argue that staff may need to focus upon particular facets of bullying in relation to its interaction with specific disabilities. Attwood (2004), for example, shows that insights about the social difficulties of young people with Asperger's syndrome, often stemming from the problems they experience in understanding the thoughts, feelings and perceptions of others, should inform the nature of the response that staff make. In Attwood's work (2004), a range of strategies were used with students with Asperger's syndrome. These included: employing a team approach among professionals; establishing a code of conduct; making a map of the young person's world; using buddy systems; and giving strategies to bystanders to help them respond effectively to instances of bullying when they occurred. Young (1998) reports, however, that other, more general, approaches to bullying, such as the support group or No Blame approach, have also been used effectively where pupils with SEN and/or disabilities are bullied.

These studies suggest that simple interventions can have a considerable impact (Frederickson 2010); and that when staff intervene, they need to think about the social experience within their schools and the social meaning of the behaviours they are targeting. This will help to shape interventions which, if they were not targeted in this way, would otherwise fail to have real impact. Peer education approaches and intervening in the peer dynamics of the classroom seem to be powerful avenues to pursue in developing interventions and these possibilities will be explored in later chapters of this book.

What are the challenges that schools face in effectively preventing and responding to this bullying?

The research suggests that schools face significant challenges in relation to bullying as it affects young people with SEN and/or disabilities. For example, schools face challenges that are associated with the logistics of implementing anti-bullying practices. The literature reveals difficulties at the level of school leadership and management; problems in implementing whole-school policy; and concerns over a lack of awareness among teachers leading to a lack of a sense of urgency in addressing the issues. In addition, there are reports of schools experiencing problems:

- detecting the existing level and nature of bullying, and monitoring ongoing occurrences
- analysing how the young people concerned perceive bullying behaviour
- attempting to use teacher ratings as well as pupils' own reports of their experiences of bullying.

Other challenges revolve around the ways in which the issue of bullying is conceptualised, particularly as it affects young people with SEN and/or disabilities. For example, some practitioners persist in viewing bullying as a manifestation of 'problem children' rather than seeking to change attitudes or recognise the crucial importance of the social context.

What kinds of studies focus on the challenges faced by schools?

Some of the studies examine interventions that have been implemented in schools and which can therefore offer practice-based perspectives on the challenges which schools face. These interventions broadly fall into two groups. On the one hand, there are strategies that focus on preventative interventions aimed at engendering a non-violent, inclusive school atmosphere: students develop generic core competencies, including non-aggressive behaviours, that they can use to deal with a wide range of issues. On the other hand, there are approaches that rely on responsive interventions: teachers use a range of strategies in order to establish and maintain a group norm regarding aggressive behaviour. These strategies include improving the ability of children to report incidents; involving support groups (see, for example, Murphy and Heyman 2007); and giving training in peer mediation (as reported by Warne 2003).

However, the literature assessing the impact of actual interventions is limited. While the last decade has seen a great increase in schools in the UK introducing anti-bullying measures of various kinds, very few of these interventions have been systematically evaluated. One reason for this is that funding for such assessments is often simply unavailable. Researchers writing about bullying also tend to be more interested in the dynamics of student behaviour than in testing the efficacy of a particular strategy. Many of the studies used for this section therefore do not address practical strategies at all, but rather are straightforward studies of the existence and nature of bullying and the victimising behaviours of young people. Nonetheless, it is possible to infer from such studies some insights into the challenges that schools might face in trying to prevent or respond to bullying behaviours that affect young people with SEN and/or disabilities.

Another feature of the research literature is that many studies focus specifically on young people with particular types of additional need or disability. Conditions that are frequently addressed in the literature, for example, include autism spectrum disorders (ASD) and hearing impairments. This means that less information is available that relates to children with other disabilities and special educational needs. This is significant because research also suggests, as indicated above, that the 'causal mechanisms' of bullying can vary according to the needs of the young people involved and the contexts in which they are situated. It may therefore be unwise to draw general conclusions from studies that have a very particular focus. Studies have also been conducted both in inclusive mainstream schools and in special schools. Bullying affecting young people with SEN and/or disabilities will occur in both contexts, but each will face different challenges in responding to it.

In the literature overall, studies tend to originate from the fields of psychology or education, and in some cases medicine, although there is some cross-referencing between studies from different disciplines. In general, there are more quantitative than qualitative studies. The quantitative studies often use sociometric measures in order to determine the relative social positions and degrees of isolation of young people, for example by asking respondents questions about who they would prefer to partner in play or work situations. Correlations with reference to the disability status of the young people can then be made. These measurement methods are often adapted: for example, in order to overcome difficulties in communicating with young people (because of their age or a hearing impairment, for instance), researchers may use cards with symbols rather than spoken or written words. Torrance (2000) argues that qualitative studies are important in trying to understand the social context of bullying. The qualitative studies that do exist tend to use observations and interviews in order to explore the perspectives of children and teachers in more depth and to attempt to interpret experiences from the participants' own points of view.

What challenges are reported at the whole-school level?

If mainstream and special schools are to implement interventions to prevent and respond to the bullying of young people with SEN and/or disabilities, then clearly additional time and resources will be required. Beyond the overarching need for more time and resources, further institutional challenges can be identified, including the need potentially to provide a range of specific solutions simultaneously while also implementing whole-school strategies.

Schools experience real tensions between, on the one hand, the drive to engender an inclusive school ethos and a general atmosphere in which diversity is valued as a dimension of ordinary life in schools and, on the other, the need to make special interventions in order to accommodate the needs of children with SEN and/or disabilities. Norwich (2008) has referred to these tensions as leading to 'dilemmas of difference' and a range of practical difficulties. In both mainstream schools and special schools, employing a number of different strategies simultaneously may be problematic. As noted earlier, although many of the 'causal mechanisms' for bullying ultimately stem from social and communication problems, schools need to be prepared to make differentiated responses for young people with different forms of additional need, and even for individual learners. Young people with either attention deficit hyperactivity disorder (ADHD) or autism spectrum disorders (ASD), for example, may be more likely to display behaviours that are perceived as aggressive or anti-social by their peers or by school staff. One study by the National Deaf Children's Society (2006) has shown that deaf children may find it particularly hard to communicate about bullying, requiring teachers to develop enhanced awareness of the issues and to create safe and secure opportunities for disclosure. Young people with learning difficulties may need staff and students to become fluent in what may be highly personalised approaches to communication in order to allow them to report and discuss their experiences of bullying. This suggests that targeted strategies will be required to prevent the marginalisation or victimisation of young people with different needs – schools will need to generate 'specific solutions for specific problems'.

In the first instance, this means that only so much can be said about challenges for schools at a general level, as different problems will emerge in relation to strategies responding to different forms of SEN and/or disabilities. However, it is clear that any school that attempts to prevent and respond to bullying for all of its pupils will face potential challenges in trying simultaneously to implement different strategies in order to address a diversity of needs. This may be particularly true in inclusive mainstream schools catering for young people with a variety of additional needs or disabilities and in mixed special schools. Dixon (2006), for example, lists the particular dilemmas facing schools implementing interventions for young people with hearing impairments. Her study shows that schools find it difficult to balance academic input with the provision of pastoral care; that tensions emerge when schools wish to enable deaf children to integrate with majority groups without forcing them to do so; and that schools have to decide whether to teach signing in all classes or only in certain designated groupings. Many dilemmas revolve around the extent to which deaf children can be fully integrated (for example, 'children's relationships can and should be improved' versus 'there are some children who just can't be helped to make friends'; 'improve communication between deaf and hearing children' versus 'communication will always be a problem for either the deaf children or the hearing children'). These dilemmas reflect some of the choices that schools have to make at both a policy level and in terms of day-to-day practice. Warne (2003), in a similar vein, lists a series of challenges facing schools implementing interventions for young people with moderate learning difficulties, identifying particular issues relating to maintaining interest in, and commitment to, those interventions and to ownership among participants of the process of implementation.

Different measures may also be required to address isolation and marginalisation, as opposed to victimisation or bullying. The two are not the same, although the former is known to be likely to increase vulnerability to the latter (see Chapter 1). Nordmann (2001) observes that the real challenge for schools lies in hearing student voices and increasing institutional participation, rather than simply reducing marginalisation. Byers et al (2008) make similar comments in the light of their work on improving emotional well-being for young people with SEN and/or disabilities in mainstream schools and colleges. Moreover, although levels of bullying of and by children with SEN and/or disabilities in mainstream and special schools is comparable (see Knox and Conti-Ramsden 2003), research suggests that different sorts of strategies may be required for each type of school. Because inclusion in the mainstream has become an increasingly popular strategy over the last 15 years, those young people who attend special schools are likely to experience the most severe forms of SEN and/or disabilities, including acute forms of social and emotional difficulty, which may require very focused and specific forms of intervention. For mainstream schools, one aspect of the dilemma of difference also appears: some forms of support and specialised intervention, although designed to facilitate integration and to promote equality in social relations, can exacerbate perceptions of difference and even lead to young people being victimised because they are seen as being in receipt of 'special treatment'.

More general efforts to tackle bullying also generate challenges of their own, since a whole-school approach of any kind demands resources, coordination and commitment. These holistic strategies are important, particularly for children with SEN and/or disabilities. Roberts (1995) recounts the disastrous consequences for her son, who has physical and mental disabilities, when his school failed to provide a coordinated response to the ways in which he was treated, particularly in terms of the bullying he experienced. When some teachers treated her son in different ways from other members of staff, the situation became confused. In addition to involving the whole school in implementing agreed and consistent strategies, it is also important to promote the participation of parents and carers, including the parents of the bullies as well as those of the bullied children.

Arguably this should, to some extent, be seen as part of the task of developing a truly inclusive mainstream school. Ensuring that young people with SEN and/or disabilities are physically present in the mainstream setting is an important first step but, by itself, it is an inadequate response. As de Monchy et al (2004) note, locational inclusion is a very basic condition and extra efforts may be needed to enable young people with SEN and/or disabilities to become part of teaching and learning groups. Further, these young people may need support in making social contacts and sustaining relationships. Alderson and Goodey (1999) offer one example of a mainstream school in which a good inclusive ethos and an effective framework of social support has enabled children with autism spectrum disorders to be socially integrated. As stated earlier, being part of a social group has been shown to reduce vulnerability to bullying – although schools also need to find ways to reduce the vulnerability of young people who do not belong to any particular group.

Despite the fact that the Equality and Human Rights Commission (2011, p.112) identifies a 'systemic institutional failure to protect disabled people' from harassment, victimisation and abuse in a range of contexts, Dixon (2006) reinforces the idea that achieving consistent results from whole-school interventions can be problematic. Much depends on the levels of support available to the school. This is especially so when anti-bullying programmes involve several different types of intervention, such as improved supervision, highly differentiated curriculum work and the development of befriending systems – interventions that may have varying levels of efficacy. Indeed, Smith et al (2004) argue that the evidence that would enable schools to identify the most effective strategies in tackling bullying is still lacking, even amongst the general school population.

What can be done to raise awareness and understanding?

A further set of challenges revolves around the ways in which bullying is conceptualised by pupils, teachers, and parents and carers, and the need for all groups to understand the social context in which bullying occurs. While challenges of this order have been noted in relation to general studies of bullying, a broader awareness of the issues is particularly pertinent in the case of bullying as it affects young people with SEN and/or disabilities. As established in Chapter 1, studies reveal that young people with SEN and/or disabilities are disproportionately vulnerable to being bullied, as well as sometimes being perceived as being bullies themselves. Kaplan and Cornell (2005) describe using a 'threat assessment' approach, which takes into account the social context of perceived threats and assesses the real level of danger they present. The authors note that when this approach is used, fewer young people with SEN and/or disabilities are excluded from school, presumably because their 'bullying' behaviour is better understood or is addressed through strategies other than exclusion. In addition, Mishna (2003) emphasises the importance of raising teachers' understanding of the impact of a young person's involvement in bullying on families, and of the need to avoid blaming the parents.

This author also states that the social context of bullying must be considered and argues that one of the challenges that schools must face concerns the process of increasing community awareness. Changes in wider attitudes will also be important in preventing the bullying of children with SEN and/or disabilities. The research indicates that schools need to re-examine the ways in which they define impairments and conditions and to scrutinise the expectations or prejudices they may have about children with particular types of SEN and/or disability. Prejudicial expectations, stereotypical generalisations and misinformation might be allowed to influence school policies so as to make them (unintentionally) socially exclusionary in their effects on young people with SEN and/or disabilities. Alderson and Goody's study (1999), for example, shows how different understandings of autism by school staff had a significant impact on the levels of social integration experienced by young people with autism spectrum disorders (ASD).

What difficulties are reported in relation to the detection and monitoring of bullying?

Practitioners are frequently reported as experiencing challenges that relate to their ability to detect, measure or monitor the existence of bullying within schools. One difficulty arises because young people with SEN and/or disabilities may fail to recognise or interpret a situation as involving bullying, even if victimisation is clearly occurring. Research by van Roekel et al (2010) found this to be the case for young people with ASD. The authors conclude that interventions that are targeted at young people with this condition should focus as much on improving their perception of bullying and victimisation as on addressing the occurrence of bullying behaviour. They suggest that young people with ASD may have particular difficulties in understanding social situations and recognising bullying behaviour. Their study indicates that, on the one hand, young people with ASD who scored highly on teacher- and self-reported victimisation were more likely to misinterpret non-bullying situations as bullying; while on the other hand, the more often adolescents with ASD bullied other children, the more they misinterpreted bullying situations as non-bullying. This sort of confusion clearly presents a challenge to schools, as it will interfere with the accurate reporting and monitoring of bullying.

In a similar study, Khemka et al (2009) revealed that young people with intellectual disabilities are not well prepared to recognise and handle situations independently when those situations involve coercion, especially coercion with a threat. These authors explored strategies through which such children could be encouraged to seek help from a responsible adult in specific circumstances.

The overall implication of these studies is that detecting victimisation that involves young people with SEN and/or disabilities can present schools with more difficulties than the monitoring of bullying in the general school population. Arguably, schools will need to help young people with SEN and/or disabilities to learn to differentiate between bullying and non-bullying behaviours before expecting them to become involved in reporting and monitoring activities.

Even in the general school population, sensitivities relating to bullying make it a difficult topic to research. Pupils, fearing recrimination from their peers, may withhold information and offer false accounts of bullying in their schools. Whitney and Smith (1993) and Dixon (2006) argue that this alone can make qualitative approaches too threatening or too inaccurate as methods to use without support from other sources. There is also the possibility that asking children about social relations may itself either positively or negatively affect the existing interpersonal context, therefore leading to inaccurate research results on the impact of interventions. This bolsters the case for using teacher ratings to help to determine levels of bullying, although, as Nabuzoka (2003) suggests, this gives rise to another set of problems.

Studies have confirmed the difficulties that exist in getting accurate reports from young people about levels of bullying. It might therefore be expected that teachers and other support staff would be well-placed to notice if a young person is being bullied and that they would act accordingly. However, research suggests that relying on teacher reports is also problematic (see Chapter 1). Teachers in mainstream schools have been consistently shown to overrate the social inclusion of young people with SEN and/or disabilities in their classes (de Monchy et al 2004); and to underestimate the degree of bullying that affects them (Whitney et al 1994b).

Some studies have directly compared peer and teacher perceptions of bullying. These studies (see, for example, Martlew and Hodson 1991, Torrance 2000, Nabuzoka 2003, de Monchy et al 2004, and Holzbauer 2008) show that, while teachers are good at knowing the numbers of friends that young people with SEN and/or disabilities have, they are often unaware of the frequency with which these pupils are being bullied or, indeed, the frequency with which they are bullying other pupils. This relates to the 'culture of disbelief' surrounding the harassment of disabled people noted by the Equality and Human Rights Commission (2011, p.54) and has been explained by referring to 'cognitive dissonance theory'. Research by de Monchy et al (2004) suggests that teachers invest significant amounts of time and energy in creating inclusive classroom environments. They keenly wish to achieve successful outcomes and therefore find it too difficult to acknowledge that the project is not working to the benefit of all children. Although one study (van Roekel et al 2010) indicates that teachers report higher levels of bullying of students with ASD than the students themselves (see above), most other studies report the opposite. It is possible that teachers may be under-reporting levels of bullying involving young people with SEN and/or disabilities either because they find it hard to believe that such bullying is happening; because it is not accepted as being a common phenomenon in schools; because feelings of guilt arise from the idea that such bullying is occurring under their supervision; or because they find it difficult to acknowledge the situation if nothing is being done to address it. Some teachers also seem to be reluctant to acknowledge that behaviours that they interpret as 'teasing' are experienced by young people as extremely hurtful and may lead ultimately to more severe forms of abuse. Whatever the speculation about causal factors, schools need to be aware that teachers are likely to under-report patterns of bullying involving young people with SEN and/or disabilities.

This is a primary challenge for schools because it suggests that staff may not be in a position to notice when a bullying situation needs to be addressed. The tendency to underestimate bullying involving young people with SEN and/or disabilities also makes it difficult to engage teachers in generating and implementing solutions. Indeed, teachers may feel anger at what seems to be implied criticism if they already feel overwhelmed by the demands of balancing different learners' needs and if they feel they have not been given the time, resources or training to deal with classroom challenges effectively.

In mainstream schools in particular, teachers have a key role to play in monitoring the social experiences of all their pupils; the social context of the classroom; and the school environment outside lessons. Arguably, teachers should be particularly alert in evaluating the social positions of pupils with SEN and/or disabilities in their classrooms, especially those who have been ignored and rejected for many years and are in danger of developing social-emotional difficulties. Pavri and Monda-Amaya (2001) argue that teachers also play a critical role in assisting pupils in acquiring social skills and in fostering social relationships by facilitating peer interactions and friendships in the classroom. However, teachers have to be aware of the need to take action before they will be prepared to take on this critical role.

Some studies have shown that there can also be significant levels of bullying in special schools, despite claims that specialist contexts can provide better levels of educational well-being than mainstream settings (see, for example, Alderson and Goodey 1999). Again, teachers may find it difficult to come to terms with this controversial finding. Torrance (2000) suggests that this might be perceived as tantamount to challenging an entire profession. While the Equality and Human Rights Commission (2011, p.111) acknowledges that there are 'barriers' to reporting and recording instances of harassment and abuse involving disabled people, barriers that might include the sensitivities of teachers, the Commission's inquiry resolutely calls for improved data on the 'scale, severity and nature' of the problem (p.167).

What main messages can be drawn from the research?

Social opportunity is an important consideration in the lives of young people with SEN and/or disabilities, since the key factors in reducing vulnerability to victimisation and bullying are social. The implication is that schools must take responsibility for promoting access for young people to social situations outside the classroom as well as to educational opportunities. The social fabric of the classroom is also important since, where there are limited opportunities for cooperative learning and friendship, there are reduced opportunities to learn social skills – and the risk of bullying is therefore increased.

There is some evidence that attending inclusive schools can help by providing opportunities for peer group association. The best factor protecting against bullying is acknowledged to be social support, provided through friendship, structured buddying or even more casual acquaintance with peers. Peer acceptance (particularly in non-classroom and playground settings) by large numbers of peers (numerous 'bystanders' rather than a few good friends) tends to protect young people with SEN and/or disabilities from bullying and victimisation. However, inclusive settings (and even schools with thoughtful anti-bullying policies) do not, in themselves, confer protection. Young people with SEN and/or disabilities may still have low social status, have few friends and be socially rejected within inclusive schools. There is also some evidence that young people with less severe special needs in mainstream schools (for example, young people with mild or 'hidden' difficulties) experience greater levels of rejection than those who have more visible forms of SEN and/or disabilities.

It is clear, then, that schools have a responsibility to focus on social issues and to teach social skills. Preventative interventions are important and can make a positive difference, especially in mainstream settings. Studies suggest that effective inclusive practices, and inclusive pedagogies in particular, can lead to lower levels of bullying by enabling students to model behaviour and by providing contexts for peer acceptance and the development of social skills.

It is also clear that interventions need to be targeted and to respond to the different challenges presented by particular disabilities. For some young people, this will mean focusing on language and communication skills. Studies have revealed that even subtle interruptions in the flow of interactions between young people with SEN and/or disabilities and their peers can lead to the exacerbation of rejection, isolation and, consequently, victimisation and bullying. Schools therefore have a responsibility to improve the work they do in the areas of language and communication. The focus should not be purely on the development of language, communication and social skills; but also on social structures, including peer affiliations and social roles. Adult roles are crucial in this, as support in the classroom needs to be carefully planned so that it does not increase isolation from peers for pupils with SEN and/or disabilities. There is also some evidence that actively teaching disability awareness, and helping young people to understand and empathise with their peers with SEN and/or disabilities, can be productive.

In addition to planning and implementing interventions, it is important to encourage all those involved (including teachers and other school staff, pupils, and parents and carers) to think through how bullying is understood and defined, particularly in terms of the bully/victim roles and the social contexts in which bullying occurs. Behaviour that demands attention, for example, includes bullying out of school and, in particular, cyberbullying. Staff, pupils, and parents and carers also need to consider how communication difficulties and (initially unintended) social exclusion can be underlying factors contributing to the emergence of bullying and victim behaviours. This kind of awareness-raising is less straightforward than more typical punishment or anti-bullying reporting strategies, and therefore may be more challenging for schools to engender, but will ultimately be more effective for bringing about a school atmosphere in which victimisation is less likely to occur.

It is evident, from the research, that interventions that are targeted at the particular needs of children with different disabilities can have a considerable impact. However, more research studies, making systematic evaluations of such interventions and their ongoing impact, need to be undertaken in order to better determine the challenges facing schools and the most effective responses that can be made. Given the current absence of such studies, in-depth work with teachers is required, especially since the research suggests that they currently underestimate the extent and severity of bullying as it involves young people with SEN and/or disabilities. Classroom staff are uniquely placed to understand the challenges that arise from bullying and from attempts to address this issue. Teacher focus groups may help, taking into account the notion, as has been suggested earlier, that bullying that affects young people with SEN and/or disabilities is likely to be a sensitive topic for them to discuss.

An important aspect of schools' approaches to bullying revolves around where the problem is located. If bullying is seen as a problem emanating from the student and their behaviour, then interventions will be deployed in the individual domain. As the literature establishes the importance of social context in the incidence of bullying, it therefore follows that prevention and responses need to focus instead on peer relations.

Interventions are reported to work in two main ways: through engaging the empathy of peers, and through engaging direct peer support. In peer groups, it is particularly effective to have open communication about special needs and appropriate responses, providing explanatory and not just descriptive information; this has been shown to increase positive interactions between young people with SEN and/or disabilities and their peers. Buddy systems and peer mediation have also been shown to be effective, and further research is needed to secure the role that participative pedagogies and peer support can play.

Studies suggest that a number of challenges face both mainstream and special schools in preventing and responding to bullying. Some challenges, such as finding the time, space and resources for professional development activities and developing preventative or anti-bullying curricula, are institutional and concern the whole school. Research suggests that particular intervention strategies may be effective for individual young people with different types of SEN and/or disabilities who are vulnerable to bullying; but identifying such strategies, adapting them if necessary and incorporating them into mainstream curricula may be time-consuming and require additional expertise and resources. It is here that external support may be particularly effective in helping schools to address this kind of bullying. At the same time, while such targeted interventions are effective, whole-school strategies also form an important foundation for these practices, and schools may find it problematic to introduce such changes comprehensively.

Another key primary challenge for schools arises from difficulties in accurately assessing the extent of bullying. Relying solely on teacher or pupil reports can be problematic: studies have shown that teachers often underestimate or have an inaccurate sense of levels of bullying; and students with SEN and/or disabilities may not recognise bullying situations, either as perpetrators or as victims. Linked to this is the issue of defining bullying: it is important for schools to have a commonly agreed definition, shared by both teachers and pupils in particular, since members of both groups are known to have differing interpretations of the behaviours they observe in schools.

It is also crucial for schools to know the extent of bullying in order to address the situation; for example, to know whether preventative programmes are enough or whether targeted interventions are required (and if so, towards which young people in particular). The challenge of generating better data may be met when school managers work with teachers in ways that are sensitive to the pressures that their responsibilities entail. The challenge is to find an appropriate and effective way of developing awareness so that teachers feel confident and comfortable about reporting incidents of bullying in their classes. This is crucial, as teachers are the adults who spend the most time directly in contact with students.

Research on bullying has begun to focus more specifically on young people with SEN and/or disabilities in the last fifteen years. Most of the studies relating to interventions suggest that, as bullying tends to occur because of peer rejection and social skills deficits, the most effective interventions focus on the psychosocial aspects of SEN and/or disabilities (as opposed to cognitive); and on how peer relations can be developed, for example, though enhancing language and communication skills among young people with SEN and/or disabilities or by actively promoting collaborative and participatory pedagogies. Accessing student views is an important first step in taking action and this suggests that further research that directly involves young people with SEN and/or disabilities would be effective.

3 The perspectives of disabled young people and those with special educational needs

Kate Martin and Philippa Stobbs

Council for Disabled Children

> *At lunchtime everybody here will be bullied. When we go out there, we'll get bullied again. Out there, as soon as you walk around, you'll get bullied.*

The extent of disability-related bullying affecting young people with SEN and/or disabilities is, far-reaching. However, as in other themes so central to their lives, there have been few opportunities provided for young people to contribute their perspectives to the debate. This chapter therefore begins with a consideration of the changing policy and social contexts that are driving a shift towards enabling their voices to be heard, before presenting some of the issues that the young people wish to be communicated to a wider audience, based on their own experiences of bullying and their views of how it should be addressed.

Despite the passage of the Children's Act (1989) and adoption and open for signature of the United Nations Convention on the Rights of the Child (1989), progress on the rights of children and young people to participate in decision-making processes has been inconsistent. The development of opportunities to influence decisions taken on their behalf has been more rapid in some areas of young people's lives than others. If education has trailed behind social care, it is perhaps because, in some schools, there is a lingering whiff of the educational philosophy of Thomas Gradgind that sees children as:

> *little vessels then and there arranged in order, ready to have imperial gallons of facts poured into them until they were full to the brim.*
>
> (Dickens 1854, Chapter 1)

Side-stepping any debate about how knowledge is constructed, nearly two centuries later, a more participative ethos means that the 'student voice' has gained prominence, with more of a focus on:

> *how students come to play a more active role in their education and schooling as a direct result of teachers becoming more attentive, in sustained or routine ways, to what students say about their experiences of learning and of school life.*
>
> (Hargreaves 2004, p.7)

However, while there has been some progress in children's participation, there has been more limited progress in the participation of disabled young people. Nine years after the Children Act was passed, Jenny Morris (1998, p.70) identified social work assessments that reported in terms such as:

She is unable to verbally communicate and therefore her view is not available.

Morris's research found that disabled children and young people were rarely consulted about their care and that, while most disabled young people in contact with social services had communication and/or cognitive impairments, social workers had rarely received training and support in communicating with them. Morris's work acted as an important spur to the development of practice in social care.

As with legislation and policy, practice in schools has trailed practice in social care; although there are signs of change. A growing body of evidence (see, for example, Lewis et al 2007) has contributed to an understanding of the importance of the perspectives of disabled children and young people in informing not just individual decision-making processes but also wider policy and practice in education. The requirement to involve disabled people in the development of disability equality schemes, a requirement under the Disability Discrimination Act (2005), provided a nudge to the system. Schools that had not previously done so started to find ways of involving disabled pupils in contributing to, and taking some responsibility for, developing better school practices; and in contributing to practices that might remove barriers to the inclusion of disabled young people in all aspects of school life.

There are legislative, moral and practical considerations that drive this imperative to hear, and take into account, young people's views. There are fundamental questions about whose school it is; how we change the ethos of schools; and how adequately we are preparing children and young people for later responsibilities in life if we do not involve them in the task of determining what sort of school they are in. This chapter is based on the premise that, of all the issues for which we need to hear, take account of and respond to the views of children and young people, bullying is surely the most personally experienced, the most potentially damaging to their well-being and therefore the one where we most need to understand what is going on. We know bullying happens but how to minimise it and how best to address it, has to be informed by the views of children and young people.

During 2010, the Council for Disabled Children consulted with over 80 disabled children and young people between the ages of 5 and 19, with a range of physical, sensory, behavioural, emotional and learning impairments. These respondents will be referred to as 'young people' throughout this chapter unless a specific case requires other terminology. They attended a range of educational settings across England: inclusive mainstream primary and secondary schools; and special schools, including residential special schools. Their quotations provide a unique insight into disabled young people's experiences of bullying and bring a challenging and persuasive perspective to the debates around these issues.

Experiences of bullying

Bullying behaviours

> *One lesson somebody behind me started flicking his pen at me and then he just kept on saying 'can I have my pen back?' And I actually did the wrong thing by giving it him back because then he did it again ... and it's still going on. They're flicking paper, rubber and I've had enough of it.*

> *I constantly got called names basically since I started school.*

> *When I fell off my bike I was like really seriously injured and everyone laughed at me and kicked me as I was on the floor.*

Like all young people, disabled young people reported experiencing a wide range of bullying behaviours on a continuum from serious incidents of physical violence to incessant occurrences of coercion, manipulation and verbal abuse. The bullying behaviours experienced by the young people involved in the Council for Disabled Children survey included:

- verbal abuse
- physical violence
- threats, fear and intimidation
- extortion
- exclusion from, and isolation within, the peer groups
- manipulation and coercion
- theft or hiding of belongings
- false friendships.

While this list of bullying behaviours may be easily recognisable, it is worth exploring how some of these behaviours affect disabled young people in particular. The young people participating in our consultation regularly stated that the bullying they experienced went unnoticed and unchallenged. They said that this was often due to bullying behaviour not being recognised by teachers as such (as certain bullying behaviours were difficult to see from an outside perspective); it becoming an 'accepted behaviour'; or, quite simply, because they were not listened to or believed when they reported incidents of it. This picture has many resonances with the picture emerging from the research (see Chapter 2) and from parents' and carers' accounts (see Chapter 4).

The majority of young people reported that they experienced verbal abuse. This abuse was not just directed towards individual young people in relation to their impairment, it also encompassed the more general and regular use of derogatory language about disability. This was reported as a feature of school life and, more often than not, went unchallenged. There was a culture of acceptance of disablist language, which affected disabled young people's self-perception, their confidence, and their ability to see the incidents as unacceptable and ones for which they had a right to report. This echoes the accepted use of homophobic language among young people in schools; and it adds weight to the importance of efforts that have been made to help young people develop cultures that are more respectful of difference (DCSF 2008b).

False friendships, and high levels of exclusion from and isolation within their peer groups were reported by disabled young people, particularly those with learning, behavioural or emotional impairments. In these instances, peers would act as if they were a young person's friend in front of onlookers, but once out of this gaze, the young person was excluded or subjected to other forms of bullying. Disabled young people reported that this form of bullying was particularly difficult for school staff to recognise because, for those looking on, friendships appeared to be in place. Disabled young people struggled to report this form of bullying because the promise of friendship (particularly for those experiencing exclusion and isolation) held a strong allure. They seemed reluctant to report the difficulties for fear of jeopardising their potential inclusion within a peer group. This was also linked to experiences of manipulation and coercion: many young people reported being coerced into doing something, such as misbehaving in the classroom or taking the blame for other children's behaviour, for the 'reward' of a friendship that did not necessarily materialise. Therefore the young person experiencing the bullying was often seen as the 'troublemaker', rather than those who were responsible for the manipulation, and was the subject of sanctions.

> You can't do 'owt really to stop it ... can't fight back ... can't tell. Makes me feel like not coming to school... don't know why I come to this school.

All of the children and young people involved in the consultation reported that they had experienced bullying, in one form or another. The level and seriousness of their experiences appeared to be strongly related to the ethos of the school and the effectiveness of the school's response, rather than the type of setting. The type of setting, mainstream or special, did not appear to correlate with higher levels of either safety or risk. What appeared to impact most on disabled young people's reports of bullying was the effectiveness of the school's response. This affected whether young people felt safe or, at the other extreme, felt isolated and hopeless about whether anything would or could be done to help them.

It is also significant that many disabled young people had experienced bullying outside school, in their community and, often, on the way to and from school.

> Sometimes people go outside your house just for fun and chuck stuff at your windows.

> Near the shops where there's like gangs that wait outside, 'n' make you give 'em your money 'n' stuff.

> Outside. In playground and out of school. Because that's the best time you can get people because there's no teachers around to stop 'em.

For young people in residential settings, bullying may happen, as a pupil at a residential school said, 'at night time'. Many school policies do not cover these out-of-school events, despite the fact that these experiences have a significant impact on young people's experiences of school – their ability to learn, and to feel safe and secure in, and part of, the school community.

Difference and disability

> In your letter there's the word disabled – you put down exactly the reason we're being bullied. The word disabled explains why we're bullied.

> They don't see the real me.

All young people related the causes of bullying to 'difference' in some form or other. However, their understanding of difference varied greatly and appeared to be strongly linked to the way in which individual schools framed this issue. It was clear from our consultation that the ethos of the school and the school's commitment to tackling bullying has a significant impact on young people's understanding of why bullying happens.

Essentially, in schools where young people felt safe, listened to, and confident in the school's response to bullying, their understanding of difference and why young people were bullied extended beyond disability. In addition, they appeared to have a much more positive understanding of impairment and disability and more positive self-perceptions as a disabled person. By contrast, in settings where there appeared to be a less effective response to bullying, disabled young people's understanding of difference and why they were bullied centred very strongly on disability alone. Young people's understanding of disability (and indeed, their perception of themselves as disabled people) was much more negative and their understanding of why they were bullied centred almost entirely on their impairment.

> Child 1: The reason [that we are getting bullied] is because you're in a wheelchair and they pick on you because you're not like them, do [you] know what I mean?

> Child 2: Yeah, and 'cos you're not like normal people. I mean we're all normal, but other people don't think so. Really, everybody's the same.

And:

> I was at school once, and they called me a word. It was spastic. It didn't bother me at first, but then a week went on and they called me it again and called me it again. Over and over.

This appeared to be reinforced by messages some had received from school staff that due to being disabled, the young people should 'learn to live with' and accept the fact that they would be bullied. As one young person reported:

> At my old school they called me 'specky four eyes' and I went to tell a teacher and they said 'just ignore it'.

Despite this, disabled young people, including some who experienced high levels of bullying, could empathise with the young person who had been bullying them and offered explanations as to why they thought this might happen. Many thought the young person who was bullying might also need help and support as, for example, they may have experienced bullying themselves or that, due to their own impairment, they may not understand that their behaviour would be perceived as bullying. The intentional nature of bullying was certainly questioned by these young people, with explanations offered such as: *'Sometimes bullies know they're bullies, sometimes they don't'*, and *'[they] Can't help it, sometimes [they] don't know it's wrong, like'*. The notion of difference was not only evident in their understanding of why certain young people experience bullying but also in their understanding of why young people, including even themselves perhaps, might display bullying behaviours.

> *Bullies are normally scared. They want attention basically, so they go and bully someone for the negative attention. They should learn to get attention for good things.*

> *I think they're bullies, cos ... like in their past life, in their last school, they could have been bullied.*

> *We're alright when we're in the classroom, but when we get out into the garden [playground] we're like, calling each other names and hitting each other, but don't think we know what we're doing sometimes.*

Effects of bullying on disabled children and young people

> *If I'm being bullied I feel like I'm in this black box and can't get out. Feel like I'm trapped in this big black box.*

Some of the young people in our consultation had been severely affected by bullying: many isolated themselves within the school environment to try and stay safe; some avoided school; and a few even said that the bullying had made them feel suicidal. Some of the young people expressed how it: *'Stops you doing stuff – [makes you] scared of going places'*, how they felt, *'Suicidal'*, or that it *'makes you want to kill yourself'*.

For many disabled young people, repeated bullying to which there had been no effective response had led them to develop a very negative self-identity, linked to their impairment. Particularly when they had been told by staff that they should 'learn to live' with bullying, their negative self-perception and identity in relation to their impairment was reinforced. This propagated an individual model of disability that located 'blame' for their experiences of bullying on the fact they were disabled; rather than on the actions of others, or on the school itself. It led many to want to give up on school altogether.

> *How can you make it stop when the bullies just walk away from the teachers? The bullies just walk away. It's just pointless really.*

As a result, many disabled young people had developed individualised and internalised responses to bullying – as if their experiences of bullying were their own 'fault' or responsibility. This was dominated by self-exclusion, where young people felt that they should remove themselves from, or completely avoid, certain situations; adapting their own behaviour and use of space, rather than believing others had a role in helping and supporting them. For example, when asked what should happen when bullying occurs, one young person in a residential special school stated that he should go *'Back to my unit. My bedroom'*. Even when asked what others could or should do to help, his answer remained the same – he saw it solely as his responsibility. This individualised and internalised response was not isolated and was a very common response from many of the disabled young people who spoke to us. This should lead us to question how our response to bullying affects not only young people's feelings of safety but also their current and future identity as disabled people.

Others also replicated this pattern of having to take responsibility themselves for the bullying, albeit in different ways. This was particularly the case for some young people with emotional and behavioural difficulties, who employed image projection as a key way by which they felt they could prevent bullying. For example, they felt they needed to present themselves as being 'tough' or 'hard' so as to deter other young people from bullying them. One young person said:

> *Have to make out like you're going to fight, even though you won't, make 'em think you'll fight 'n' they won't bully you.*

Reporting bullying when it happens

> *If someone is bullying you, then tell your teacher 'n' they sort it out. They just … sort it out.*

> *It can be hard to tell because you might be upset, and you might not wanna tell anyone 'cos they might think you're like, weak.*

> *Grassing makes things worse – makes you scared to tell – like blackmail.*

Feeling able to report bullying when it happened was a significant issue for disabled young people. Their willingness 'to tell' varied greatly from school to school: it apparently related to whether they felt anyone would listen; whether they would be believed; and whether the school would be able to do anything to stop the bullying.

Fear of retribution

One of the key issues that prevented disabled young people from reporting bullying was the fear of retribution or exacerbation of an already difficult situation; as one young person expressed, *'If you tell, they'll beat you up more.'* Many young people felt that reporting bullying would simply make the situation worse and thus they chose to endure it, particularly if they had been instructed to keep quiet and threatened with consequence for not doing so. For instance, some of the young people said:

> *The people being bullied would be even more upset because the bullies would be bullying them extra, because they would have to go somewhere … to like a detention after school.*

> *You can't do anything about it. You can't tell. Two reasons – 1 … you don't know their name [said due to size of the school], so they'll get away with it; 2 … you'll get bullied even more 'cos they'll call you a grasser.*

I've heard that often bullies use death threats like 'if you report me, I'll kill you'.

I get that [death threats] all the time.

Even where disabled young people wanted to report incidents of bullying, many struggled to do so. This was particularly so in large secondary schools where, as the quote above also reveals, due to the number of students, young people often did not know the name of the perpetrator, so were unable to report them.

There's these gangs that hang around the back of the sports hall and you go around there, and you get, erm, threatened 'n' have to run away. There's places you can't go. Like [another child] said, even if you did tell, you don't know their names; you don't know who they are.

I got bullied, and I didn't know who it was, so they got these photos so I could recognise her face.

Not being believed

They don't always believe you when you tell.

The truth is that many teachers never realise how serious a situation is.

Another key concern and experience of many disabled young people was not being believed, and this affected their willingness and confidence to report bullying. This was particularly common amongst young people with learning difficulties or autism spectrum disorders (ASD). As mentioned previously, many disabled young people reported that, due to being disabled, they had been told, by school staff, to expect bullying or to learn to live with it. In addition, even when disabled young people did report bullying, they often reported that teachers failed to listen; respond effectively; or discuss what response the young person would like to the situation. For example, many young people wanted support from the teacher to try and talk with the other young person, resolve the situation and ultimately make friends: but they reported that the teacher often just issued a sanction, which was ineffective and often exacerbated the problem. This has obvious consequences, as the young people said:

Makes upset when don't listen what say. Upset.

Upset ... we're trying to tell the truth, but then we get in trouble for lying and they [the bully] get nothing. It makes me angry.

There are further serious consequences for disabled young people. In particular, it shapes their interpretations of school as a place of safety:

School's hardly safe because ... if all the bullies get away with things and I don't then school is by no means a safe place.

Moreover, when disabled young people were not listened to or believed, they reported that they were significantly less likely to try and talk to an adult about bullying in the future; this then led to internalising of bullying, making it 'their' problem to solve. What young people really want is the knowledge and reassurance of having someone who will believe them and act on what they have to say and, in some cases, this has not always been a class teacher.

> *Child 1: The teachers don't sort it out. The TA [teaching assistant] does though.*

> *Facilitator: What's different about the TA? What does she do differently?*

> *Child 1: She does something about it … teachers don't take any notice … she listens.*

> *Child 2: She listens to us, finds out what we want … then goes and sorts it out in our way.*

Retaliation

> *I just got so angry I couldn't stand it anymore, so I just hit them.*

Many disabled young people, particularly those who experienced high levels of bullying without an effective response, spoke with desperation about how they felt pushed to their limits by repeated, unchallenged incidents of bullying. When eventually they retaliated through sheer frustration, they reported that they were the ones who then got into trouble and were subjected to sanctions, with no action being taken against the perpetrators.

> *I've been excluded when really they were far more in the wrong than me.*

> *I got excluded because all the winding up like, it got … it happened so often that I just got really angry and couldn't control myself anymore. Eventually I ended up taking my anger out on someone … and as a result I ended up getting excluded … because I was considered a 'health and safety matter' by the school.*

However, some young people, in the face of the lack of support they experienced, saw retaliation as their only hope of stopping bullying.

> *End up retaliating – gets you in trouble, but stops 'em bullying.*

> *If you sit there 'n' take it they'll do it more – gotta fight back and they'll stop.*

Disabled young people's views on how to improve prevention and schools' responses to bullying

Preventative measures

Disabled young people spoke with passion and maturity about understanding and valuing difference and disability as effective ways of preventing bullying occurring in the first place. They proposed responses to bullying that looked beyond the specific act or incident, and which focused on enabling young people to understand each other and work to develop a friendship or mutually agreed solutions. Disabled young people strongly believed that if other young people were supported to understand and value difference and disability, this would be an effective way to prevent 'disablist' bullying:

> *Right, I forgot what you call it, like disabled stuff. Like more people with different abilities so people would understand more.*

> *I think adults and young people should be more understanding and maybe have more awareness of disabled people, 'cos at the moment I don't think they are aware. It's so simple, you just have to teach them one time and it will stay with them forever.*

Prevention might include disability awareness and equality training; lessons for pupils, teachers and support staff; positive images of disability within the school setting; and the positive portrayal of disability throughout the school curriculum. Disabled young people were keen to be involved in these ideas and work in partnership with school staff, to raise awareness of disability equality and bullying in particular. In addition to preventing bullying, they also felt this would develop the confidence of disabled young people and enable them to develop a positive self-identity, and awareness of their right not to be bullied.

> *Could do like, an assembly or play about bullying and disability … Or a rap. Should show it to everyone.*

> *I want schools to take bullying more seriously – disabled children are more vulnerable to bullying. Teachers could teach classes about disability … disabled kids could help if they wanted to. A bit like a new lesson!*

Disabled young people spoke passionately about the need for all young people to be aware of what bullying is; the rules about bullying within the school environment; and what they should do if they witnessed or experienced bullying, including the use of disablist language. Being clear and explicit about the topic was welcomed.

> *I think it was about two years ago, I was in school, erm, I think they got a PowerPoint or whatever 'n' they gave a question about someone being bullied 'n' gave you a few choices – Do you … do you laugh 'n' join in? Do you get a teacher? Do you stop it yourself? … Do you walk away?*

They felt strongly that all young people should be involved in developing these rules, so that they understood them and felt ownership of them – making it more likely that they would be adhered to. This participative approach was not only restricted to improving behaviours among pupils, but also extended to educating teachers.

> *We would be the adults for the day, and tell the teachers what they should do better.*

The young people believed that the rules about bullying should be highly visible around the school; and be presented in accessible formats (such as using pictures and symbols) to ensure that all young people could access them, understand them, and know they have the right to be protected from bullying.

Other solutions addressed the high levels of exclusion and isolation within their peer group that many young people spoke of, such as initiatives to support, develop and sustain friendships which would prevent bullying from reoccurring. Some young people spoke of Bully Buddies – young people who buddy another pupil to prevent them from feeling isolated and excluded, to support them in developing a friendship group, and to build their confidence and self-esteem. Many disabled young people also valued having supervision outside lessons; or a key individual that they could trust for support. This reassured them – knowing there was someone there to turn to if bullying occurred – and they felt this deterred other pupils from bullying them.

They'd keep an eye on everything ... to make sure we don't get bullied.

Evident throughout all their suggestions was the desire of disabled young people to work in partnership with school staff and non-disabled pupils, to prevent and respond to bullying. Their practical recommendations included setting up anti-bullying committees; training teachers and pupils to understand disablist bullying and to develop a positive understanding of disability; and taking on numerous different roles, such as peer mentors or bully buddies.

Responding to bullying when it happens

On the whole, disabled young people strongly supported and preferred a graduated, non-punitive or non-sanction-based response to bullying. Most thought sanction-based approaches often made the situation worse and created a fear of retaliation, making the perpetrator more likely to rebel against the imposed sanction. Neither did they feel that such approaches addressed what they perceived to be the real underlying causes, such as a lack of understanding about disability. What they really wanted were constructive solutions that enabled young people to understand each other and develop friendships; and the provision of help and support for the young person who had bullied. This was a majority opinion: the only exception to this was in cases where the bullying was long-term and all other approaches had failed, that is, where young people who had experienced long-term, severe bullying had reached breaking point.

Disabled young people also identified peer mentoring and peer mediation as two key methods of responding to bullying. They felt that peer mentoring could provide them with the support they needed when bullying occurred; they were also keen to act as peer mentors to other pupils, to enable them to raise awareness of the issues faced by disabled pupils and to share their personal experiences for the benefit of others.

Peer mediation was regularly cited as a valued way to enable pupils to deal with bullying incidents. With the right training and support, disabled pupils felt able to support other pupils to resolve issues; and strongly valued being able to do so. They felt that, with support from their peers, they could talk to the bully and would therefore be more likely to reach a shared agreement, understand and value each other, and to develop a friendship as a result.

Child: What we did in my primary school about bullying, we did this peer mediation thing, where there were two people, the bully 'n' the one being picked on, 'n' if they had like a fight, we would sit 'em down 'n' let them decide what they thought they could do to sort it out.

Facilitator: Why do you think it worked so well?

Child: Because if you just tell 'em what to do, they often think that: 'I don't wanna do that' 'n' 'It's unfair', whereas, if they decide together, they can, like, form it as an agreement. I was a peer mediator 'n' it was really good 'n' if there was like a lot of 'em fighting I would take some 'n' my partner would take the other 'n' let them decide 'cos if you forced them to do something it might just aggravate 'em 'n' it'd carry things on.

Many disabled young people also spoke about the need to know they have safe places to go to when bullying occurs. These included areas of the school where supervised activities took place during break times. Just the existence of these safe places gave young people reassurance, whether or not they decided to use them.

They could have some rooms, which if you're bullied you can go to and you can do some stuff which will calm you down … like a game.

In my school, nowhere's better because there's just so much space that the bully can just follow you everywhere.

In addition, young people wanted to know where to go to and who they could talk to when bullying occurred. This could be somewhere they could talk to fellow pupils or school staff. Positive and trusting relationships with school staff were a key feature of most of the suggestions made by disabled young people. They needed to know that they could have time to talk when they needed it, and that staff would listen to them and believe them. One young person described such a supportive individual in their school:

She's the only one that understands us and what we're saying. All the other teachers think we're messing about or joking about or lying to them. She knows us … she knows us pretty well, and knows we're not lying.

When staff failed to listen, this prevented disabled young people from reporting bullying. In some schools, young people spoke positively about their school having an 'open door policy'. They had developed positive, supportive relationships with school staff and knew that they could, at any time, approach a member of staff and be given the time to talk. In addition to knowing they would be listened to, children and young people needed to know they would be believed and given the time and space to explore their feelings about the bullying incident. As one person said, 'It makes you feel better inside' [being listened to].

Some young people said that sometimes, even though something had upset them, they might not know if this was classed as bullying. Further, they might not know how to resolve this with the other pupil, and they felt they needed the space to talk this through with a member of staff.

When reporting bullying, disabled young people wanted time to agree, in partnership, the appropriate response. They felt that responses should be personalised to the particular situation and to the young person's wishes. Many young people said they just wanted to know they could talk to someone and learn how to challenge bullying themselves at an early stage, yet they feared that, if they told, a sanction for the bully would automatically be incurred. Young people also valued staff for their support in mediation. Mediation provided the opportunity to talk about the bullying incident in a safe environment, to understand each other, and agree an effective solution.

> She called me a cripple. I told my mum and she spoke to the school. They sat us down together and we could talk about it. I think it helped her to understand why I got upset.

The disabled young people spoke in a very mature way about the need for support, both for the young person who has been bullied and for the young person who has bullied. They understood that, often, young people who bully may have problems themselves and need support to understand what they have done and to change their behaviour. In addition, disabled young people sometimes felt that sanction-based approaches worsen, rather than rectify, situations. They therefore felt that supporting the young person who has bullied to understand their behaviour and its consequences was potentially an effective first step.

> Maybe they could give them some sort of rehabilitation class in the detention. [to enable them to understand their own behaviour]

Positive approaches were preferred over punishments.

> I've got another thing for a reward thing, it's like you get stamps, and when you get a certain amount of stamps you get a merit and what you could do is you could get a card if you'd been reported to bullying, and you could get a stamp if you didn't bully, you'd get a big reward.

This view extended to the need for support to enable disabled young people to understand their own behaviour. Many disabled young people told us that sometimes they did not understand that their own behaviour could be perceived as bullying by other young people. They wanted support from school staff to learn about and understand how their behaviour could be perceived by and affect others. Some children and young people, particularly those with autism, also reported difficulties in understanding whether particular behaviours were bullying or not. This reduced the likelihood of their reporting it.

> Some jokes are quite nice and some jokes are not nice and that's why I didn't know.

Support was expressed for helping all the individuals involved to better understand the way actions are interpreted.

> When they're bullying sometimes they don't know its bullying and people just say this is bullying so they don't really understand what bullying is. They need to understand how it makes the person they're doing it to feel. They need to be told how it feels.

In fact, young people with behavioural difficulties arising from an impairment, and whose behaviour could be perceived as bullying by others, were very aware of how their behaviour could affect other young people. They wanted to be involved in helping other young people to learn about their behaviour and to understand that it was linked to their impairment, rather than necessarily being intentional; to know that '[they] can't help it, sometimes don't know it's wrong like'.

Some young people told us that they had developed agreed ways of responding, for example, when they have reported an incident of bullying: a teacher or teaching assistant would check with them discreetly every day by giving them a 'thumbs up' sign.

> Thumbs up, means things've been good, thumbs down mean it has been bad.

If the young person responded with a 'thumbs up' – everything was fine, but if they gave a 'thumbs down', then the teacher made sure that they had time later on to talk through what had happened. This reassured young people that someone was there for them, they were not isolated in dealing with bullying, and that they were in control of the situation and the responses being made.

Conclusion

It is worth noting again the depth and maturity of disabled young people's views and recommendations that was evident throughout the research. Disabled young people proposed many ways in which bullying could be prevented and responded to more effectively. There were clear messages from young people that they wanted to be fully involved in making change happen. They wanted to be partners in change, rather than being the passive recipients of policies and systems designed and imposed on them by others. They were concerned that such approaches did not take account of their actual and lived experience of bullying.

The young people's views identified in this chapter make a significant contribution to our understanding of how we should prevent and address bullying. It is also worth noting that, all too often, these very same young people were routinely denied the opportunity to share their views and experiences in the very place it matters most: their schools. Each school needs to be engaged in hearing directly from the children and young people who are part of that community. Importantly these young people reflect as much on how schools handle disability and difference as they do on how schools handle bullying.

It is clear that if we are to tackle bullying effectively, we need to shift from a position that views disabled young people as the victims of bullying and who regularly have systems and policies imposed upon them – to empowering disabled children and young people to be partners in change, enabling them to share their views, experiences and their recommendations for a better future. They are, after all, the ones who live this experience; they are the experts in their own lives. Without their participation, existing and future policies, systems and approaches to bullying will continue to fail and to disempower disabled young people; further, disabled young people will internalise responses to bullying and develop negative self-identities. We need to empower them to develop their confidence, self-esteem, identify positively as disabled people and feel they are equal and valued members of their school community.

Acknowledgement

With thanks to all the children and young people who took part in the Council for Disabled Children survey, who so willingly offered their views and shared their experiences.

4 The perspectives of parents, carers and families

Claire Pimm

Contact a Family

> *It is hard to express just how awful the whole situation was and the problems that it still brings us – five years on*
>
> (Parent of a bullied child)

Bullying is one of the most difficult experiences a parent or carer of a child with SEN and/or disabilities can experience. They already face a unique combination of emotional, social, physical and financial pressures that impact on their family lives. For example, they may struggle to come to terms with the news of a child's disability; experience poor health exacerbated by caring responsibilities; or struggle with a lack of time for themselves and each other. Other problems arise from balancing the demands of work and caring: finding appropriate childcare, arranging for flexibility in working patterns and getting regular time off, all of which potentially increase the risk of hostility from colleagues. There may also be financial pressures due to the additional costs of raising a disabled child. Parents and carers often report feeling that they experience a lack of support and understanding from professionals and the wider family network and community. This is compounded by feelings that professionals do not act on their concerns about their child's development; that there may be a lack of suitable services; and that it takes considerable effort to access those available. In the face of these wider contexts, the additional stress of having to deal with the bullying of a child at school can be considerable. How effective the responses to bullying episodes are can have significant impacts on family life.

Chapter 4 reports on the findings of a survey conducted with parents and carers of children with disabilities by Contact a Family (a voluntary organisation aimed at supporting families with disabled children). The survey was conducted online between January and April 2011, using the organisation's Facebook page, with the key aim of accessing parents', carers' and families' views about their experiences of bullying at school. In total, 80 parents and carers of disabled children completed the survey, the majority of whom have children with disabilities (62 per cent); 35 per cent have a child identified with SEN; and 3 per cent have both. Parents and carers participating in the survey completed the survey anonymously; so there was no need to disclose where their child attended school or whether it was a mainstream or special school.

The key themes raised by the survey will be highlighted here, presenting parents' and carers' accounts of their experiences of bullying, in relation to their children, as returned in their survey responses. It also considers the impacts of bullying incidents on their children and families; and presents the parents' and carers' accounts of how the bullying has been dealt with in schools (both more and less successfully). Of course the results demonstrate a degree of voluntary response bias, because almost all of the responses were received from parents and carers who had a vested interest in responding as a result of their own child experiencing bullying (96 per cent of respondents). This notwithstanding, parents and carers participating in the survey expressed a considerable strength of feeling around this issue which it is important to communicate: many felt an overwhelming sense of anger, sometimes even several years after bullying events had occurred. There is also considerable overlap and resonances with the experiences reported by the children in Chapter 3.

This chapter attempts to present as many of these perspectives as possible and it is worth emphasising that many of the parents and carers involved welcomed being able to participate in the research. They felt it important to point out that they feel that the issue could have been handled more helpfully by schools. Recommendations from parents and carers on how bullying could be dealt with more effectively when it occurs in and around the school environment are included.

Types of bullying experienced

As discussed in more detail in the Chapter 1 (see 'What kinds of bullying and victimisation are reported?'), bullying, or unkind actions which are repetitive and difficult to stop, can take a multitude of forms. These include verbal; emotional; physical; sexual; and racial bullying. Amongst the parents and carers who responded to the survey, the most common form of bullying experienced by their children was verbal (36 per cent), followed by emotional (30 per cent) and physical (28 per cent), with 2 per cent of respondents reporting either sexual or racial bullying. Other forms of bullying identified by parents and carers accounted for 3 per cent of responses. These included being excluded from taking part in activities; cyberbullying; stealing and damaging personal property; and parent-led bullying.

The survey was directed primarily at understanding experiences of bullying in school and it also focused typically on child-to-child direct and relational bullying. However, it is also worth emphasising that, for a number of the families, their child's experience of bullying had also occurred out of school, especially when the other children involved lived nearby. Parents and carers also reported that their children had experienced cyberbullying when they were at home. Finally, a small number of families reported bullying (or perceived acts of bullying) being carried out by other adults rather than children, including other parents or teachers.

> *Our son has been ... ridiculed, humiliated in front of peers, treated differently, punished for incidents that is not proportional to the incident that has occurred, physically threatened and isolated by teachers.*

> *The parents of the two children concerned told the school they objected to the presence of an autistic child in their children's class.*

Although this was only reported by a small number of families and therefore not considered in great detail here, it is nevertheless an alarming issue, for which more awareness is required.

The nature of bullying experienced and its effects

Identity-based bullying

> *My daughter had people brush her 'germs' off each time she touched them or brushed past them and her friends were told she was contagious. She was also ridiculed by others as she changed, as she struggles to dress.*

A very important issue to emerge from the research with parents and carers is that, for a high proportion of respondents (85 per cent), bullying experienced by their children was perceived to occur as a consequence of their having disabilities or special educational needs. Being disabled in and of itself was reason enough for some pupils to bully another child, with the 'difference' present in their child's appearance or behaviour providing the explanatory factor as to why they were targeted by bullies. This chimes with the findings of the Equality and Human Rights Commission's inquiry into disability-related harassment in general (2011). One parent felt that their child was bullied *'because my child is different from the other children in her school'*; while another commented that, *'the bullies expressly said this is why they were treating him in the way they were'*.

On one hand, the responses show that difference itself provokes bullying: for example, one parent explained how their son's *'poor coordination gave bullies something to target'*; while another young person's behaviour was seen as *'provocative'* because of their different characteristics, such as misreading social cues or being *'too loud'* (see discussion in Chapter 6). On the other hand, bullying situations were also reported as being provoked or exacerbated by the children's differences in ability to respond to the aggression of others. For instance, they may have problems in perceiving appropriate behaviour and in identifying bullying; may be less able to argue back or stand up for themselves; or may have limited ability to communicate and report the problem in the same manner as other children would, which could lead to an escalation from low-level behaviour to more serious problems. In these cases, parents and carers revealed that they felt their child's disability hindered their capacity to appropriately respond, as others would, to potential bullying situations.

> *He sees everyone as his friend, even when people are hitting him.*

He is vulnerable, non-verbal and not able to report an issue.

Because he can't get away fast as he is in a wheelchair.

According to the parents and carers, it is clear that there are inherent vulnerabilities in simply being a young person with SEN and/or disabilities at school that places them at risk. However, there are also differences created regarding communication, physical abilities, and ability to understand social situations, that are perceived by parents and carers as rendering these children more vulnerable still.

Effects of bullying on disabled children and young people

The stories emerging from investigating parents', carers' and families' perspectives confirm a distressing picture of incidents, which often had serious impacts on the children involved. In one case, a parent reported that her daughter *'had to go to A&E due to injuries she received at school'*; while in another case, a parent reported that her son felt he was left with no alternative but to attempt suicide when responsible professionals failed to respond adequately. In these accounts, the effects of disablist bullying were wide-reaching and damaging for the children and young people, with consequences and knock-on effects lasting far longer than the bullying itself:

He was bullied unmercifully throughout primary school, which resulted in his being verbally aggressive and occasionally physically violent. It destroyed his self-esteem and resulted in self-harming.

As this case demonstrates, and as has been explored previously, there is sometimes a blurring of victim and perpetrator roles, in which the child who was originally bullied adopted those same tendencies themselves. Again however, as confirmed by the testimonies of children themselves, when the disabled children retaliated against bullying, parents and carers reported that it was their child who became subject to accusations of bullying. In some cases, this led to the permanent exclusion of the child with disabilities or SEN. One parent reported how this potential outcome itself became a motivation to report the bullying incidents:

[There is a] tendency to disbelieve or victim blame. [I] found it important to tell them [the school] regardless, otherwise he would have been seen as the troublemaker when he reacted/retaliated.

Feelings of injustice, when a child who was bullied then retaliated, also came through in a number of accounts.

Not one child suffered an exclusion for a physical assault but my son did when he assaulted another child after much provocation.

They said it was a two-way thing.

Addressing problems at an earlier stage would prevent this escalation of events. However, the difficulty of children revealing bullying only through aggressive retaliation highlights the complexities around the issue, particularly when communication of bullying is not easy or straightforward for these pupils. Some parents and carers commented, for example, on how:

> He used to come home so upset but couldn't explain to me what was going on. It took days for him to tell me.

> He would often come home from school moody and unable to express what happened.

It is clear that these types of problems require highly responsive procedures for detection, and necessitate sensitive handling. Teachers and support staff in schools need to be alert to the different ways in which the issue may manifest itself – even through aggressive behaviour towards others – and consider how such events may be communicated differently among children with SEN and/or disabilities.

Identifying and responding to bullying

Finding out

Parents and carers in the research told of how they became aware of the bullying in many different ways, through a multitude of channels and on different occasions. For just over half of respondents (51 per cent), parents and carers were told directly about the bullying by their child. In other cases, school staff members informed them (9 per cent); another pupil told them (7 per cent); another parent informed them (6 per cent); a sibling told them (6 per cent); or it was reported by the Child and Adolescent Mental Health Services (CAMHS) (1 per cent). Parents and carers also found out about the bullying through other means: including witnessing it happening (9 per cent); and detecting it through noticing the wider effects or consequences of the bullying (7 per cent). It is important to note that in only 13 per cent of the cases did families report that they were told about the bullying by school staff or teachers, and this reinforces important questions raised elsewhere in the research about how school bullying is identified and monitored.

Next steps: school responses

Nearly all of the parents and carers (99 per cent) reported the bullying to the school (the remaining 1 per cent did not because another student had already done so). It was most commonly reported to the headteacher (33 per cent); followed by the class teacher (26 per cent); special educational needs coordinator (SENCO) (19 per cent); form tutor (10 per cent); and school nurse (1 per cent). Some 12 per cent also reported the problem to other sources, including school governors, parish priests, head of year, and children's services coordinator. In 6 per cent of cases, the bullying was reported to a number of different sources, usually because it was felt that the situation had been ignored or not dealt with adequately by the initial contact person. Some parents and carers said they had reported it to as many as five official sources. Schools reacted in a variety of ways once the allegation of bullying had been made; however only 22 per cent of families felt that the school had been effective; whereas 68 per cent reported that the response from the school was poor and unhelpful.

In terms of positive responses, the families offered a number of approaches that they had felt addressed the problem well. These included direct action involving the individual pupil identified as a bully; wider processes of educating children in the school about their child's disabilities in the school or class; the establishment of a range of support mechanisms, including peer support; and, above all perhaps, the use of good communication between school and home. In terms of less helpful responses, parents and carers revealed issues including schools: downplaying or denying there was a problem; locating it as their child's 'fault'; not responding in any effective way or indirectly penalising their child instead through the 'solutions' offered; and not keeping parents and carers informed. In these negative instances, parents reported considerable and sometimes dramatic consequences, including having to home-educate their child or take legal action.

Positive responses

A number of families who had experienced effective responses highlighted the importance of specific, direct action undertaken with the alleged bully to address their behaviour. This was usually experienced as a member of the school staff speaking to the other young person, for example: 'the Head spoke to the pupils concerned'; and, in another case, a teacher who 'spoke to the bully and explained about it not being nice bullying another child'. Other strategies included physically moving the bully to another class; while in another case, 'they [the bully] were named and shamed'. These strategies seem to appeal to parents and carers as they offer them a resolution, with clear sanctions applied to discourage the behaviour. This sort of resolution appears to be important in other cases, for example one parent discussed how the school had also involved the child's mother.

> She approached me to apologise and told me that the boy would be punished at home by having no treats, TV or computer time for a week.

Another effective response identified by these parents and carers was felt to be that of educating pupils in school or class around their child's disability. This involved pupils being explicitly confronted with awareness of the disability, with the aim of improving their understanding and empathy for the student.

> They did an education session with the rest of the class on autism to increase awareness and make sure everyone was aware of appropriate behaviour.

> They read a story about a child in a wheelchair, placed a poster outside the class of a child in a wheelchair and gave the children the opportunity to help my son and become part of his routine.

This fostering of understanding in the school community was also mentioned in another case, whereby school personnel '*invited an expert into the school to better understand my son's conditions and how to minimise his reactions*'. It could also be developed explicitly through other mechanisms or school procedures, for example through encouraging peer protection. Parents' and carers' accounts mentioned circle of friends, buddying systems and personalised communications.

> *They involved inclusion support staff to set up a circle of friends [a structured programme with six to eight volunteers who create a support network for the child; provide encouragement and recognition for progress made; work with them to identify any difficulties; and devise and implement practical ideas to deal with difficulties] to ensure he has safe friends who he could trust and who would not stand by while this was happening.*

> *[Staff] put a buddying system in place so she was accompanied from lesson to lesson and she was given access at any time to the learning support base.*

> *[Staff] shadowed my son to ensure it was not continuing to take place.*

> *[Teachers] gave my son an exit card to show when he is stressed in class.*

What can be seen from many of these accounts is the importance of clear communication and a jointly agreed strategy to tackle bullying, in which parents and carers are involved along the way.

> *The teacher has been very supportive and is totally aware of the situation and keeps me updated.*

> *The school held a meeting between us, the class teacher, the school counsellor, and a psychologist to discuss ideas to help my son.*

These examples are in stark contrast to other cases, for example that recorded by Roberts (1995, p.26) and accounts later in this chapter, where schools' confusion in response and lack of a holistic and coordinated approach to cases of bullying are experienced as very distressing by parents and carers.

Good practice was also noted in the consequent treatment of the child, wherein they are supported, encouraged and not treated in any way as if they are at fault.

> *The most useful thing they [the school] did over the next couple of weeks [after the bullying was reported] was to ensure that his self-esteem was not damaged in any way … they made sure they praised him for all the good things he did.*
> (Contact a Family, February 2010)

In summary therefore, according to parents and carers, the most effective responses were seen to be direct action with the bully; fostering awareness among the peer group; and strategies to encourage peer group support and communication. It is also evident that parents and carers need to feel that they know what actions are being taken to tackle the bullying, as seen for instance in staff directly working with the bully to address their behaviour.

Negative responses

Despite the evidence of some supportive practice perceived by parents, families and carers, it is striking that 68 per cent of families felt that school responses had not been effective and were in some cases rather negative or unhelpful. Among responses deemed unhelpful were those where the parent or carer is not taken seriously or believed when reporting bullying to the school. Many parents and carers in the survey experienced schools denying the occurrence of bullying, or downplaying its severity. As one family reported, the school 'brushed it under the carpet'. Others stated that:

> At first [the school] denied it, then admitted it was happening, but did nothing about it.

> They wouldn't believe us or our boys and insisted they don't have bullying in their school.

> They refused to believe us, claimed we were lying and subsequently excluded our son due to his reaction to being bullied.

> The primary school at which my son used to go were at first quite dismissive. This was until my son tried to hang himself at the age of 11. They then started to take a bit more notice.

Downplaying the significance of bullying was also achieved by locating the problem in the victim's alleged lack of resilience. For example, one parent reported how, 'they said he had to get used to it as all children would be called names'. Indeed, for many parents and carers who repeatedly drew attention to bullying, they felt that they themselves were also treated as troublemakers, causing unnecessary problems.

> Very quickly we felt we were becoming a nuisance. 'What's the problem this time?' was a comment from a teacher on a few occasions... Some instances necessitated the need for the involvement of the police. We became so desperate after our last meeting with the Head, he admitted that he couldn't guarantee our son's safety whilst at school!

In a significant number of cases, parents and carers reported that the school did nothing at all when they reported bullying. This may indeed be the actual outcome, or it may simply reflect that parents and carers were not informed of whether and when actions had been taken to address the issue. In other cases, actions were apparently taken which had only superficial effects, leaving the real damage to go on.

> [They] Investigated it, accepted it happened, apologised for it but at the same time allowed it [to] continue.

In either case, this response was felt by parents and carers to cause considerable frustration and unhappiness; with parents and carers left in limbo, worrying about the safety of their child at school.

Another troubling response for parents and carers were cases where they felt their child was being penalised instead of the aggressor. In some instances, this outcome arose out of genuine, well-intentioned desires to keep the child safe, but the wider ramifications were that the child felt they were being punished instead of the bully.

> *Their solution was to keep him in a break times and lunchtimes so he was not exposed to the other children.*

These sorts of solutions can lead to considerable feelings of injustice for parents and children.

> *Why should a child with disabilities not be allowed to go outside during free time because the school cannot control the actions of the other children?*

The perceived unhelpful responses of schools left many families feeling angry, frustrated, powerless or unsupported. As parents expressed, the school responses were felt to be:

> *Totally ineffective and we were made to feel the onus was on us and not for the school to deal with.*

> *Defensive and unhelpful.*

> *very attentive at the time, but nothing constructive ever seems to come from it. No updates, no follow-ups. Passed from one person to another.*

Moreover, parents and carers often reported further knock-on effects arising from unhelpful school responses, which further compounded or exacerbated the negative consequences of the actual bullying incidences. Children's trust in others can decline, or indeed if the bullying is not carefully monitored it can escalate in severity following a complaint.

> *My son will now not go to school staff when there's a problem as he says there's no point as they never believe him and nothing gets sorted.*

> *[The] bullying got worse but turned from physical bullying to emotional bullying.*

Another reported how the perceived unhelpful response from the school had 'made my son feel more worthless'.

Resolutions

Finally, parents and carers were asked their feelings about how the matter was resolved. Many parents and carers (55 per cent) were very unhappy with how the situation had been dealt with. Only 17 per cent were happy with how the issue had been resolved; and a further 28 per cent of respondents 'do not know'. The high rate of incidences of those saying they 'do not know' possibly alludes to the fact that many of the cases are ongoing, and may take months and in some cases years to resolve, as the following responses testify.

> *Matter hasn't been resolved yet and is ongoing.*

> *it is still on-going, the bullying continues…*

Even in cases where a resolution has occurred, some parents and carers still spoke of metaphorically 'walking on eggshells', as one said, 'We are happy for now but always waiting for the next thing.'

It was obvious that, in a number of cases, parents and carers were so unhappy with how the situation had been dealt with that they felt forced to take stronger action. Some took their child out of school as a result. Some moved to mainstream schools and some to special schools.

> Nothing was achieved and luckily my daughter was moved out of county to a specialised school for her.

> Not great, as my son no longer attends mainstream education.

> I moved my child to another school. There they act on bullying as soon as they are aware of it. The difference in my child was remarkable.

> We took our child out of school in desperation and for his own well-being.

The levels of frustration and efforts required to effect change were remarkable, with parents and carers in some instances having to engage in legal action, complaining to authorities and finding their own solutions.

> It wasn't resolved but did form part of our legal case to have him placed elsewhere.

> I tried everything – including calling in the exclusion/inclusion officer for the local children's services partnership and complaining to the Governors. I ended up having to remove him from the school part way through year 6.

Such efforts place a considerable burden on the whole family, including siblings. Parents and carers, having to resort to more drastic measures, reported being under increased stress and having their employment opportunities damaged as they felt no alternative but to engage in home schooling or lengthy processes of appeals.

> I took my son out of school and contacted the county. Their response was slow and my child was out of school for a long period of time. He now attends a school for the recovery and rehabilitation of severely bullied children.

> We've ended up home schooling our son. I've had to give up my career and stay at home to look after him.

In some cases, the effects are devastating.

> My son became progressively more damaged, became a minor bully himself and I nearly had a nervous breakdown.

Conclusions: moving on

The testimonies of parents and carers reveal that, while bullying of their children with SEN and/or disabilities is always distressing, the responses of schools can influence the extent of the damage significantly. In the minority of cases, schools were felt to be offering helpful solutions. The majority, however, felt that the responses offered were ineffective and that there was much more that schools could and should be doing.

Tables 4.1 and 4.2 present some of the recommendations that parents and carers raised.

Parents and carers advise teachers in dealing with this issue to take the following steps. (For brevity, this table uses 'parents' to mean 'parents and carers'.)

Table 4.1: Guidance for school practitioners

1. **Listen to the person reporting the bullying** Parents stress that it is essential that if their child reports bullying to another adult in school, the appropriate response of the teacher is to believe that they are telling the truth. The consequences of a child reporting bullying to an adult at home or at school and feeling that they are not listened to or believed are damaging and far reaching.

2. **Listen to the parents** Parents are the experts in their child's behaviour and disability and know when something is wrong. Parents are usually the first people to be either told about the bullying or spot the signs of it through changes in their child's behaviour. When they report bullying to the school, they want to be believed and listened to, not labelled as 'causing trouble' or being 'overly sensitive'.

3. **Listen to both sides** Recognise that bullies often have their own problems. Parents know that many children deal with difficult situations and that their bullying may be a consequence of feelings provoked by other wider events. They want all children to be listened to and supported.

4. **Develop good communication** Parents believe this would help to solve the distrust between parties involved in these situations. It helps all those involved to feel that they are working towards a solution, even when this takes time. Developing good communication applies to all the people involved, that is, between parents and school staff, between pupils, and between the parents of the child suffering the bullying and those carrying out the bullying acts.

5. **Respond quickly, once a concern has been raised** Many parents reported investigations that took many weeks or months, during which time the child may continue to be bullied or be excluded from activities. This often left parents feeling 'in limbo' and as though nothing was being done. It is important that some tangible action or investigation is seen to happen.

6. **Take action against the bullies** Many parents reported that nothing had happened once they had raised a concern and that no actions were taken against those who had been bullying. Parents suggested appropriate actions could include speaking to the individuals, getting them to acknowledge their actions and apologise; or for the bully to be moved into another class. Other possible actions could be for teachers to use warnings and exclusions (selectively), so that the bully knows they cannot continue with this type of behaviour. Some actions may only need to occur once, and others may require longer term support.

7. **Use active support techniques** Support the child by, for example, using the circle of friends; a buddy scheme; and safe zones, for when the child is distressed or needs some time alone. Other suggestions include the use of communication cards, which a child in class can use to let the teacher know if they are upset, feeling stressed or in need of support or time out; and offering support to the child in corridors, which would ensure that bad behaviour does not occur between classes.

8. **Have a positive school-wide ethos towards all forms of disability** Actions could include running awareness sessions on different types of disabilities and the behaviours associated with them, and encouraging better understanding of how and why different people behave in different ways. This could be facilitated by bringing experts in to talk to the school; or getting students to study famous people who have had a disability.

9. **Be seen to actively discourage bullying** Run a range of school-wide activities: discussions in class; question-and-answer sessions; projects on bullying and its effects; and anti-bullying assemblies.

10. **Ensure that all teachers and staff have training in disability awareness** Include guidance on spotting the signs of bullying, as well as techniques for managing the situation when it occurs. Guidance on how to effectively offer support to those involved would also be helpful.

11. **Develop effective and well-publicised policies on dealing with bullying** Get all children, staff and parents to sign up to them. Make them an essential part of the school's Code of Conduct, as well as the discipline and behaviour guidelines. All parents should be made aware of these in order to know what their opportunities for recourse are if they are not happy with the ways that the policies are being implemented. There should be opportunities for regular monitoring and reviewing of these policies, involving parents and children, including those with disabilities and Special Educational Needs.

12. **Offer help for the parents and siblings to cope with effects of the bullying** This could include better signposting to local and condition-specific support groups and links to parent/carer forums.

13. **Educate the wider community** Include other parents, so that they better understand disability and difference.

This section presents a number of recommendations made by parents and carers, in order to guide other affected parents and carers on what they could ask the school to do if their child is experiencing bullying.

Table 4.2: Guidance for parents and carers in approaching schools

1. **Have a named person your child can tell about the bullying** This could be their teacher, support worker or SENCO. Make sure your child knows where they are in the school and how they can find them.

2. **Have a safe place your child can go to during breaks or lunchtimes** This may be a quiet area, a designated classroom or the library. Make sure the lunchtime supervisors are aware of this provision.

3. **Create a sign or signal your child can use** This is for use at school, to communicate with staff if they need to leave the room or feel distressed.

4. **Take responsibility for the behaviour of pupils beyond the school gate** This especially relates to behaviour on transport to and from school.

5. **Provide training** Give school and local authority staff training in special educational needs and disabilities.

6. **Be aware of unstructured times** Lunchtime, breaks and when moving around the school are potential times of risk for bullying to occur. These times are not always covered in statements or coordinated support plans, yet support is often needed for young people with SEN and/or disabilities then.

7. **Do not remove the child who is being bullied from the situation** Remove the child who is exhibiting bullying behaviour instead.

8. **Encourage communication between teaching staff and lunchtime supervisors** This ensures that both are aware of what could be happening in the playground and classrooms.

9. **Provide a safe area of the playground** This will enable young people to feel secure, for instance provide a zone where there is more supervision than in other areas.

10. **Allow children the opportunity to stay indoors during breaks** For example, set up lunchtime clubs and activities.

11. **Provide support at times of transition** This would cover moving from primary to secondary school; or moving from a special school or unit to a mainstream school.

12. **Use the SEAL programme** Otherwise known as the Social and Emotional Aspects of Learning programme, this is a voluntary programme for schools that is designed to develop the social, emotional and behavioural skills of all pupils.

13. **Use the 'Circle of Friends' programme** This is a structured programme, based on the concept of six to eight volunteers creating a support network for the young person; providing encouragement and recognition for progress made; working with them to identify any difficulties; and devising and implementing practical ideas to deal with difficulties.

14. **Review the anti-bullying policy regularly** Involve parents, carers and pupils in the reviews, including disabled young people and parents of disabled children.

15. **Work on social skills** Work with pupils on practising letting other people speak first, listening to other people's opinions without reacting aggressively, and understanding body language.

16. **Give praise and encouragement** Give this to the young people involved.

5 The perspective from practitioners and schools

Caroline Oliver, Colleen McLaughlin and Richard Byers

University of Cambridge, Faculty of Education

The research and personal testimonies raised in *Perspectives on Bullying and Difference* thus far indicate that there are considerable challenges faced by schools in responding to this form of bullying. The way in which schools respond to 'difference' and the bullying of children with SEN and/or disabilities significantly shapes children's experiences: it has the potential to constructively help or, in some cases, unintentionally exacerbate the problem. The stories from parents, carers and young people (Chapters 3 and 4) highlight some difficulties, such as children not being believed or being blamed for bullying, or schools not always being effective in communicating with parents and carers. Such a picture is troubling, but nevertheless this chapter explores evidence from schools and allied organisations that demonstrate some creative and supportive responses to the bullying of young people with SEN and/or disabilities. This chapter therefore gives voice to practitioners within schools who are currently developing their own initiatives to confront and respond to this type of bullying.

In beginning to understand 'what works', our intention was to explore some of the interventions that are already used within some English schools and associated agencies. The chapter draws on a national call for validated practices that respond to this form of bullying (for methodology, see Appendix 2). The intention was to offer a snapshot of how some schools, teachers, local authorities and other associate professionals deal with the problem. Equally, we aimed to assess how far – or indeed whether – the responses are known to be effective. A central aim of the research was to establish how confident teachers can be that their interventions *work* in eliminating this type of bullying.

This chapter gives a broad account of the variety of practices that practitioners shared, and considers both the potential benefits and implications of employing the interventions suggested. It also gives a number of in-depth case studies, offering a picture of where practices have been used to good effect. The final section of the chapter offers a discussion of teachers accounting for their approaches' effectiveness. While we found among teachers that there was often genuine belief in the value of the practices, a significant conclusion is that they lacked robust evidence or any rigorous evaluation of their practices to demonstrate their impact. Though they felt the strategies were helpful, it is clear that there is considerable work to be done in developing a comprehensive research programme to evaluate effectiveness, as well as establishing a warrant for practice that can be used by practitioners to demonstrate how well their approaches work in dealing with this form of bullying.

Background and context

Much of the research into bullying assesses 'within child' character traits demonstrated by the bully and the victim. As important as such studies are, this individualised psychological approach used alone risks underestimating the wider social contexts in which bullying takes place (Yoneyama and Naito 2003, Faris and Felmlee 2011). As noted in Chapter 2, however, there has been a significant shift in the literature towards conceptualising bullying as located in the social contexts of schools and young people's lives (see, for example, Luciano and Savage 2007). In particular, school and classroom factors – such as the influence of a school's environment; its ethos; the social hierarchies of pupils; interactions between peers; staff attitudes; and discipline models – are all important in shaping the likelihood of, and responses to, bullying of all pupils (Farrington 1993).

Recent years have seen encouraging signs of change in school approaches to dealing with violence and bullying more generally: for example, anti-bullying schemes are now commonplace and Anti-Bullying Week a nationwide event. However, there is less evidence of how effective such general anti-bullying approaches are for more vulnerable students, particularly those students who are 'different' in some way – as a result of their race, sexuality or disability – who are known to suffer higher levels of bullying (Tippett et al 2010). As noted by Luciano and Savage (2007), thoughtful anti-bullying policies or an inclusive approach in schools does not necessarily confer protection for these pupils. And there is often minimal awareness of the issue: a recent analysis of 217 school anti-bullying policies showed that only 15 per cent referred to disability-based bullying (Smith et al 2008).

Our task therefore was to identify and probe interventions that are currently being used in schools in England to respond to bullying among children with SEN and/or disabilities. This was not necessarily straightforward. First, it was not easy to generate responses: perhaps because we asked not only about interventions but also about how and whether they were proven to be effective. This also suggests that there may be too little specific practice addressed towards this type of bullying. Our research team also found that, while many schools have anti-bullying strategies, there were fewer responses that directly, rather than indirectly, aimed to tackle this specific problem. Rather, schools tended to adapt their generic strategies on an ad hoc basis when problems arose for children with SEN and/or disabilities.

Nevertheless, following the call for validated local practice on this issue, we were able to work with a number of teachers and related practitioners from a variety of schools, local authorities and voluntary organisations. They came forward to share 23 examples of what they felt worked in addressing this problem in their schools and agencies. (For further details of methodology and participants, see Appendix 2). The discussion here represents their combined efforts to interrogate their own practices for effectiveness. It is important to point out that what is offered here does not, by any means, suggest the problem is solved. Rather, it indicates some hopeful areas for further work.

What responses are there to bullying among children with SEN and/or disabilities?

Practitioners shared a multitude of approaches which, for purposes of clarity, have been organised into four categories (A–D) and eight 'interventions' (1–8). An important caveat is that in practice, these approaches overlap, with multiple interventions employed in one site. Not all of the approaches are exclusive to tackling bullying relating to SEN and/or disabilities. Instead, they are often embedded in other more generic approaches to tackling bullying and improving inclusion, for example those aimed at a better understanding of others and the encouragement of healthy and positive social relationships. The box below lists the interventions shared with the research team.

Interventions shared by practitioners, listed within categories

A: External approaches (often at the level of the local authority)
1. General preventative training and awareness-raising
2. Monitoring of bullying and SEN and/or disabilities for policy work

B: Environmental context approaches
3. Improvements to environment and contexts

C: Social context and peer group approaches
4. Development of a whole-school ethos
5. Raising awareness and understanding of young people with SEN and/or disabilities
6. Preventative and reactive small group work with peers to resolve bullying incidents

D: Approaches that empower and equip the individual to address bullying
7. Individualised support and counselling
8. Confidence raising and skills training

Each type of intervention will be outlined in brief, with reference to real-life examples shared as part of the research exercise; followed by more detailed case studies of good practice. Immediately after each theme of intervention – external, environmental, social and individual – we consider to what extent the examples of current practice are considered effective by practitioners. A flexible interpretation of the term 'most effective' is used here because effectiveness can be identified across a variety of dimensions, not merely relating to the reduced frequency of bullying behaviour but also to wider issues such as improvements in reported emotional well-being, and enhanced resilience or social participation. Despite a wealth of data, we have some further observations to make on the challenges of validating practice. This emerges from the finding that participants could offer only limited clear data on the effectiveness of strategies.

Category A: External approaches

The first type of interventions shared with us were support services, training and monitoring practices offered by the local authority.

Intervention 1: General preventative training and awareness-raising

Many schools made use of specialist teams of dedicated anti-bullying personnel from their local authorities, who delivered generic or tailored training to staff. In addition to other regular anti-bullying work, some cases referred to specific sessions on bullying relating to young people with SEN and/or disabilities or to other specific aspects of bullying (for example, cyber safety or homophobic bullying). In some cases, training was also provided around preventative strategies (such as lunchtime supervision – see Intervention 3); and responsive strategies (such as peer mentoring/mediation – see Intervention 6).

In addition to the delivery of such programmes in schools, the schools and local authorities provided examples of larger 'one-off' events, where specialists presented information or generated discussion with teachers about bullying and related topics. For example, Newcastle local authority held an awareness-raising conference aimed at professionals in schools, social care and health settings, which explored the topic of bullying of young people with SEN and/or disabilities. Other schools had local authorities deliver sessions on wider initiatives such as the *Social and Emotional Aspects of Learning* (SEAL) (DCSF, 2007), Unicef's *Rights of the Child* (United Nations, 1989) and Nasen's 2010 initiative *Breaking down Barriers* (see http://www.nasen.org.uk). While these events do not directly focus on bullying and SEN and/or disabilities, they were presented by participants as generating the sorts of environments in schools, and the types of attitudes among pupils that would reduce the likelihood of pupils engaging in identity-based bullying.

There were other ways in which local authorities worked with schools on the issue. Essex local authority, for example, held training sessions with SENCOs on how to make anti-bullying policy and practice relevant to those with SEN and/or disabilities. Some local authorities also provided bespoke support and guidance tailored to the needs of the school so that if, for example, an incident arose in which disability-related bullying was a problem, they would be called in to offer advice or tailored services (often using other interventions presented later in this chapter).

Local authority initiatives were also supplemented by events run in schools, including events organised by outreach teams working between special and mainstream schools. Project work during anti-bullying week and other specific times may also have been directed towards this issue. For example, in one school, activities were carried out during anti-bullying week to allow students to try to experience what it would be like to have dyslexia.

Case study 1: Newcastle County Council

Newcastle County Council's RESPONSE anti-bullying team offers a range of interventions and support to young people and families in respect of bullying issues. One such initiative was their hosting of a *Special Educational Needs and Disability Bullying* conference at the Newcastle Assembly Rooms in 2008. The aim of the conference was to highlight some of the issues around bullying and disability; identify current legislation and guidelines to support vulnerable young people and their families; and to explore good practice. Professionals from education, children's services and health attended the day, while young people from local schools were involved in the planning and delivery of the event. One of the key recommendations of the conference was the need for more awareness-raising work in schools about disability-related bullying (see Intervention 4).

RESPONSE subsequently developed a number of sessions, which were then delivered in schools. They use DVD and case studies to tell stories of young people experiencing disability-related bullying. Through activities and using age-appropriate literature, they encourage young people to think of ways to make their school more inclusive and to develop strategies that will enable them to effectively challenge disablist bullying. Post-event evaluations have been positive and will inform future practice.

Intervention 2: Monitoring of bullying and SEN and/or disabilities for policy work

This type of intervention was focused on monitoring bullying and was, again, an initiative coordinated by local authorities. Data was collected, year on year, on the frequency and nature of bullying incidents occurring within schools, for example recording cases of SEN and/or disabilities-related bullying and homophobic bullying. Some local authorities were piloting specific software – such as the *Sentinel* database for recording, monitoring and tracking incidents in schools – which allowed for effective comparison across schools.

This specific monitoring was one way of making the problem of disability-related bullying more visible, rather than submerged within the wider issue of bullying. Related to this were other attempts that some local authorities made to raise the profile of SEN and/or disabilities related bullying through specific tailoring of anti-bullying policies, via consultation with SEN Coordinators and/or disabilities advisors, behaviour support workers, specialist teachers, and parents and carers. Other ways in which awareness of the problem has been heightened is through some local authorities' specific accreditation of schools' anti-bullying policies, where schools were required to show evidence of how they took account of disability and the needs of vulnerable groups in the formulations of their policies. Furthermore, some local authorities offered anti-bullying awards, which encouraged schools to develop and gather evidence of good practice.

Case study 2: East Sussex local authority

East Sussex local authority monitors all referrals to the anti-bullying team for SEN and/or disabilities. They have found that their local figures 'would appear to mirror the national trend with children and young people with SEN and/or disabilities disproportionately more likely to be referred to the Anti-Bullying Team than their non-disabled peers' (East Sussex Anti Bullying Team 2010, p.7).

On the basis of their monitoring, the local authority became aware that their existing anti-bullying strategies had not always proved successful for children with SEN and/or disabilities. They judge their work as successful if bullying of a child stops within three to four weeks, with no repeat event within three months. Figures showed that 86 per cent of their work is effective by these standards. However, their team recognised that the minority for whom it was less successful was for young people with SEN and/or disabilities. As a result, the anti-bullying team developed an adapted toolkit for one-to-one support applicable for these young people; and developed systems for schools to report and record incidents consistently.

The toolkit utilises a solution-focused approach to be used by children with SEN and/or disabilities, as well as by siblings, parents and carers of the child, where necessary, to reinforce or reassert their anti-bullying strategies. The toolkit has sessions tailored to the children's special educational needs and/or disabilities: for example, using communication in print; or working with children with ASD on building up peer support and friendships, which are recognised as essential protective factors against bullying, but known to be problematic among this group of young people.

How effective are external approaches?

External approaches by local authorities (Interventions 1 and 2) were generally well evaluated by practitioners, because they support teachers in confronting the issue of bullying in relation to young people with SEN and/or disabilities. The use of small specialist teams from outside schools to deliver training, to ensure that school policies responded to the issue and to keep a wider eye on the problem through monitoring, were seen to signal a local authority's awareness of this type of bullying. They also helped by strengthening existing anti-bullying programmes; fostering the development of inclusive attitudes among pupils in schools, and providing extra support for schools when the issue arises. Evidence of the effectiveness of these approaches was in the form of post-event evaluations, which showed that training days were well-received and appreciated by teachers and pupils. They were seen to offer welcome informal spaces to raise sensitive issues and also to raise awareness of how, why and when this form of bullying occurs (see also Intervention 4).

However, it was clear that post-event evaluations tell us little of the actual impact in terms of longer-term reduction of bullying. In this respect, some participants raised fears that one-off and short-term approaches were limited in how far they could address the complexity of some manifestations of bullying. Such concerns were raised by representatives from local authorities, who expressed that they were limited in how far they could work intensively with schools because of resource and capacity limitations. Other downsides were that at events run by the local authority, it was not always possible to know how many pupils with SEN and/or disabilities the teams were addressing, and people delivering the events felt limited in their ability to gain detailed awareness of individuals' particular difficulties. This restricted their ability to offer the intensive one-to-one support that they felt might be required. Given that bullying is such a sensitive topic to raise for students, participants questioned therefore whether one-off events got to the heart of the problem. However, these types of intervention did appear to have a wider benefit, that of promoting an awareness that may ultimately help a problem to be aired, as well as equip teachers with some knowledge of how to respond.

There was stronger support for monitoring disability-related bullying: the mandate for which is strengthened by research demonstrating that part of the problem in adequately responding to bullying among children with SEN and/or disabilities is that the phenomenon has been significantly underestimated (Frederickson et al 2007, Hanish and Guerra 2000, Pepler et al 1994, Sharp 1996). Self-evaluations by practitioners suggested that monitoring offers a means by which anti-bullying work can be data-driven and responsive, especially when trends are observed through collection of year-on-year data and around specific types of bullying. There were even cases identified where specific types of bullying have been reduced: monitoring in one local authority had shown an increase in racist bullying, and more careful monitoring of subsequent incidents lead to a significant decrease.

Monitoring nevertheless still relies on teachers' self-reporting and this may be problematic because of the known prevalence for under-reporting (see Olweus 1978, Besag 1989, Martlew and Hodson 1991). Moreover, it relies on additional auxiliary strategies: used alone, it yields solely data and therefore does not necessarily lead to effective responses unless those data are used as part of a wider strategy, for example to evaluate the effectiveness of other anti-bullying interventions. One local authority spokesperson in this study reported, for example, that there was not enough action taken on the data: 'measuring impact is not embedded in much of the activity, especially because many are individual initiatives'. Monitoring also relies on consistent reporting locally and can be difficult to embed because it is centrally driven rather than owned by schools. Other local authorities reported that they did not use monitoring specifically for SEN and/or disabilities, because it was not felt to be a high enough priority. Nevertheless, having reliable information on the scale and nature of the problem, in clear communication from schools, is seen as a very important foundation for adequate responses. In fact, it has been a fundamental aspiration arrived at from advocacy work around this topic, as demonstrated by Mencap's commitment to embed adequate monitoring, emerging from its (2007) *Don't Stick it, Stop it! Campaign.*

Category B: Environmental context approaches

These types of intervention address physical and environmental changes that can be made to inhibit the possibility of bullying.

Intervention 3: Improvements to environment and contexts

These types of initiative focus on altering the physical and social spaces in which bullying episodes take place, and work on improving pupils' experiences in playgrounds, around schools and during break times. Strategies involved peer or staff monitoring or surveillance: ranging from the use of dedicated anti-bullying monitors patrolling the playground; to adopting a 'zero tolerance' philosophy around bullying, whereby CCTV is employed and severe punitive action taken when bullying is observed. Other strategies included creations of 'safe zones', quiet zones and vulnerable students' lunchtime clubs; the availability of form rooms during break times; and the provision of anonymous reporting stations, where cases of bullying could be confidentially reported. They could also be used in conjunction with other interventions involving the peer group (see in particular Intervention 6). For example, where anti-bully playground monitors discovered incidences of bullying, group strategies would be subsequently used to seek resolutions.

Other initiatives focused on altering experiences of 'play', recognising that often bullying, particularly in primary schools, develops out of play experiences that get out of hand. It might involve, for example, the training of lunchtime supervisors; the high visibility of staff; and the development of playtime projects, such as 'positive playtimes' and inclusive play.

Other schools offered other creative solutions by altering young people's experiences of spaces and times in the school day in which bullying often occurred. Some examples included reducing the time for lunch breaks to diminish opportunities for bullying, or identifying and adapting environmental 'hot spots', such as toilets, to make them safer spaces.

Case study 3: Bottisham Village College

Bottisham Village College secured a £15,000 grant from the government's TaMHS (Targeted Mental Health in Schools) programme and developed a number of action research initiatives. Vulnerable pupils approaching transition from primary schools were consulted. They identified bullying as a key concern in approaching transitions, especially because of an ongoing myth that children were often thrown into 'the prickly bush' in the school grounds. Students in Years 7, 8 and 9 made a video with professional help to address these pupils' worries and students were trained to show the videos and do circle work in the primary schools. Vulnerable prospective pupils were also invited into the school in the summer holidays, to familiarise themselves with the grounds through fun events such as a treasure hunt. Parent information evenings were also established to help manage parents' and carers' anxieties about issues such as travelling on the bus.

Second, in English lessons, students used the textbook *Kingdom of the Sea* (by Robert Westall) to discuss perceptions of safety, and mapped where they felt safe and where they did not in the college. It emerged that Year 7s felt genuinely unsafe in the toilets, and this issue was brought to school council through student voice. The college is due to launch a trial of a 'Year 7 only' toilet in the brand-new block, so that new students feel safe and unthreatened.

The college collects data on effectiveness because they will be required to demonstrate outcomes to their funders. They are able to show before-and-after information from a variety of sources to demonstrate effectiveness, including: maps of the school detailing pupils' perception of safety; post-event evaluations; and comparisons of a follow-up survey with baseline data from their health-promoting behaviour survey.

Effectiveness of environmental context approaches

One of the central benefits of environmental approaches was that they tended to be responsive to students' concerns about their environment, and yet were also relatively simple and low-cost solutions, requiring only minimal adaptations on the part of schools. Suggestions raised by students, for example through action research projects and consultations, often required very minor changes to be made, which nevertheless had real impacts on student perceptions of safety. Where these environmental changes were responsive to students' concerns, they also had additional benefits in building students' confidence and engendering a sense of empowerment. However, they rely on schools having well-established channels of communication and can do little to address forms of bullying that occur in non-physical spaces, such as cyberbullying, for which children with SEN and/or disabilities may be potentially more vulnerable. There are also resource implications, as some of the initiatives require training (that is, for lunchtime supervisors – see Intervention 1), which would involve extending contracts and require further commitment from school employees. This is also the case in strategies such as the use of anti-bullying patrols, which requires ongoing training for students and effective adult support to ensure responses are proportionate, appropriate and informed.

Category C: Social context and peer group approaches

Intervention 4: Development of a whole-school ethos

The next level of intervention, which was part of a number influencing the social contexts of schools, was possibly the most important school intervention, one on which the success of many other school-based interventions rested. The development of a whole-school policy was not exclusively aimed at addressing bullying and SEN and/or disabilities, but was nevertheless seen as fundamental to creating an inclusive environment in which bullying would be less likely to flourish. The approach rested on commitments to a number of principles, including open communication strategies; 'joined up' practice across staff groups to deal with problems; embedding holistic strategies; using a non-punitive approach in relation to bullying; positive modelling of behaviour by staff; and a focus on children's individuality. It was felt that these commitments would create calmer environments in schools and that pupils would feel able to report incidents through the development of an open 'telling environment', without fear of exacerbating a situation. Such an approach sees bullying as a systemic problem rather than an individual one, and one which requires intervention directed at the whole school (Smith, Schneider et al 2004).

Case study 4: Oak Field School and Sports College

Oak Field is a Special School that is engaged in 'lifetime' work to foster an 'anti-victim' mentality among its pupils with SEN and/or disabilities. The school aims to empower students from nursery onwards and has a philosophy of encouraging them to develop a strong sense of self-worth. They aim to help their students avoid adopting a victim mentality, whereby they 'allow' things to happen to them. Young people with SEN and/or disabilities at the school learn to gain insight into their behaviours (which can also be beneficial in helping children who are at risk of becoming bullies themselves). The school has spent twenty years developing a programme including language, communication and emotional work; verbal and non-verbal signals (such as bodily demeanour, clothing choice and deference to others); and addressing weaknesses typically exploited by bullies. Role-play is used to enact events so that young people with SEN and/or disabilities, many of whom are visual learners, can learn about the justice and injustice of situations.

These attitudes are not only cultivated in relation to school contexts but also prepare young people with SEN and/or disabilities for local community situations where bullying is likely to occur. The school challenges avoidance strategies that are common with people with SEN and/or disabilities, instead encouraging their pupils to go out to events, theatres and sports to learn to cope in real-life situations. It is a very broad and holistic whole-school approach, covering work with parents, families and carers who have learning difficulties as well as involving collaboration with local day services.

Intervention 5: Raising awareness and understanding of young people with SEN and/or disabilities

This intervention was aimed at altering young people's social contexts by awareness-raising projects. It aimed to develop more understanding among non-disabled children of the experiences and perspectives of children with disabilities. Such strategies were based on the expectation that fostering this type of knowledge would increase empathy and reduce children's ignorance; and that miscomprehension often informs bullying episodes. Most of the interventions involved some kind of project work, which could be run by schools themselves or by voluntary organisations.

Examples offered to the researchers included several projects that aimed to generate relationships between young people with learning difficulties and those without. Some employed a task, such as making a film about experiences of young people with disabilities, which helped promote awareness. Other examples were fundraising projects, such as where a year group in a mainstream school had to raise £2,000 for a wheelchair for a young person in the attached specialist unit with muscular dystrophy (that could raise him to a standing position). As part of the process, the young person explained to his non-disabled peers why he wanted the chair and how this would improve his life. By doing this, the mainstream students learned a great deal about life from that young person's point of view. A similar approach was also adopted by some voluntary associations, whereby representatives came into schools to give information to groups of pupils about the nature of a specific disability (such as facial disfigurement or ASD) prior to a pupil with SEN and/or disabilities starting a new class or school. While these approaches make 'special' needs more explicit, central to these approaches is the encouragement of empathy – the ability to put oneself in another's shoes.

Case study 5: Grapevine's 'We're all the same' project

The project, We're all the same, was established by Grapevine, a locally based voluntary organisation in Coventry. It was conceived on the basis of evidence obtained anecdotally, and from questionnaires given to young people without learning difficulties about their perceptions of people with learning difficulties. These suggested that the two groups of people rarely spend time together. The project was established to overcome this social distance and to foster cohesive relationships between young people with and without learning difficulties. It involved advisory groups, 'myth busting' workshops, the creation of a DVD and a shared holiday.

The Grapevine project was evaluated using pre- and post-intervention questionnaires about the perceptions of young people with learning disabilities. Evidence of efficacy was suggested via positive feedback from the young people involved in the project (including letters from family members and other stakeholders); and via attitudinal changes among students who had formerly held negative attitudes. Further evidence of success is seen through the fact that, because firm friendships were developed, the advisory group maintains sustained contact with Grapevine three years after the project has finished. The project was positively evaluated for involving the wider community, thereby reaching a wider target group than can be achieved by working in schools alone.

Intervention 6: Preventative and reactive small group work with peers to resolve bullying incidents

Another strategy that was raised by many practitioners was the establishment of small groups of students to work either preventatively or reactively to address bullying. This practice included the establishment of nurture and transitions groups, which were used for vulnerable groups of students to ease their move from primary to secondary school. During the groups, staff used supplementary techniques such as skills and confidence work with the young people (see Intervention 8). Other versions that fostered support among peers were buddying systems and peer mentoring, whereby selected group of friends were assigned to 'look out' for vulnerable children. More specific actions included the use of ABCs (anti-bullying councils).

Small group work that had a more reactive aim was found in interventions such as support group or solution-focused and/or restorative justice approaches. These relied on collaboration among peers to problem-solve and repair conflict situations within safe environments. A wider approach to encourage students to openly express feelings about difficult events, was the 'circle of compassion' or 'circle of friends' approach, whereby the peers of a young person experiencing distress or difficulty were engaged in problem solving.

Case study 6: Quintin Kynaston

Quintin Kynaston School is a large school in Westminster, with a student support faculty devoted to dealing with personal, emotional and relationship issues among pupils. Staff members supporting this work include a clinical psychologist, nurse and psychotherapist. Multiple group sessions are offered, on an 'as needs' basis, including groups on: restorative justice; emotional management; transition; speech and language; think first; and social communication. There are also nurture groups; circle of friends; circle time; family group; and Inclusion Voice, a novel initiative where students with SEN and/or disabilities are supported in making contributions to their school's 'student voice'.

Group sessions are based on therapeutic listening and cognitive behavioural therapy, dealing with issues including anger management, emotional management, relaxation, social skills and emotional resilience, often with the support of families. Many sessions reinforce what to do in general when a student is being bullied but others, such as restorative justice sessions, more specifically respond to actual bullying incidents. The interventions are evaluated using pre- and post-intervention measures by participants or facilitators on their behalf. Staff feedback is also used to assess the effectiveness of interventions through regular referral meetings. The group work is part of a whole-school approach.

Effectiveness of social context and peer group approaches

The types of intervention aiming to improve the overall social contexts and social relationships of school pupils were seen by practitioners as highly positive, perhaps chiefly because the results are seen in tangible improvements in students' interpersonal relationships. These group approaches are evidence of a shift towards the recognition of the importance of psychosocial aspects of SEN and/or disabilities, and the role of peer relations in preventing and responding to bullying (McLaughlin et al 2010a). Project work that aims to raise awareness, wider whole-school initiatives, and small group work among peers that aims to improve the social fabric and develop inclusive practices all appear to offer significant positive experiences for those involved.

In particular, whole-school interventions are also seen to be absolutely crucial by students themselves: the consultation with pupils with SEN and/or disabilities (Chapter 3) revealed that the degree to which pupils felt they were believed, and were responded to, when they reported bullying is important for any pupil – and whole-school strategies aim to create the conditions in which this is possible. The positive evaluation of this type of initiative by practitioners was informed by anecdotal evidence (participants' viewpoints of observed improvements in relationships; letters from satisfied parents and carers of young people with SEN and/or disabilities; teachers noting calmer classrooms; and children making good progress in their studies). However, there has been some independent evaluation of contributing initiatives to a whole-school ethos, such as the Unicef *Rights of the Child*. Brighton and Sussex universities' evaluation suggests that in the schools considered, 'there was little or no bullying or shouting'; an improvement in positive attitudes towards peers with disabilities; and a challenging of externally imposed stereotypes or prejudices (Sebba and Robinson 2010).

Moreover, awareness-raising through project work and so on was reported by the practitioners as leading to better tolerance among the young people involved and reduced conflict within classrooms. It was also seen to produce important changes within the young people – both those identified as having SEN and those not – such as improved feelings of self-esteem. The exercises offered informal learning opportunities for mainstream students; and challenged the misunderstanding and ignorance that often forms the root of disability-related bullying. The interventions were not always considered to be leading to participants developing long-lasting friendships with young people with SEN (although sometimes they did) but nevertheless, they were seen to have other important ramifications, such as encouraging non-disabled peers to challenge bullying as bystanders. This viewpoint is reinforced by research evaluating this type of programme (see Chapter 2); for example, Saylor and Leach (2009) researched an initiative which brought peers together for shared arts, sports, camps, service and leisure activities and concluded that this led to increased empathy between those with and without disabilities and a decrease in bullying.

In the case of peer group approaches, our interventions fall into two main approaches. First, some groups provided opportunities for students to develop friendships (such as nurture and transition groups), thereby providing protective resources against bullying. Second were groups that functioned more reactively, dealing with actual bullying incidents and breakdowns in interpersonal relationships (such as restorative justice approaches). These were approaches that aimed to exploit children's understanding of their peers and their own abilities to conceive of imaginative solutions. Effectiveness was measured by pupil perception scores taken before and after group interventions, although personal testimony was also offered as evidence of how effective these approaches were in eliminating bullying.

The literature-based research shows that there is a growing body of evidence for the effectiveness of peer education. Researchers have explored a number of these approaches specifically, including buddy systems (Frederickson 2010); Circle of Friends (Etherington 2007); and peer mediation (Warne 2003). As noted in Chapter 2 however, there is little rigorous evaluation of these programmes and little detail about how they are managed with children with SEN and/or disabilities (Moore 2009). A recent review of the effectiveness of group interventions with particular groups of pupils suggests caution when working with some groups together, such as anti-social young people, particularly because of the possible unintended peer effects (see, for example, Farrington and Ttofi 2009). Similarly, there were also concerns raised by practitioners that some peer initiatives, such as anti-bullying councils, were variable in outcome because of the difficulty that 'it is only as good as its participants'. Teachers' experiences revealed these initiatives as time-consuming, requiring both time for training and ongoing support for the pupils involved.

For both whole-school and awareness-raising approaches, committed and responsible leadership was essential. As noted in the literature review, a whole-school approach of any kind is not without difficulties and 'requires resources, coordination and commitment' (McLaughlin et al 2010a, p.37). If the approach is only partially embedded and not all staff members are totally committed to the idea, bullying incidents are likely to recur. This was seen to be particularly likely if groups were run by external agencies (such as voluntary groups or local authorities) and schools did not take ownership of the problem. As noted in the literature review and reinforced by wider research, 'the effectiveness of individual and peer support interventions depends in part on whether they are supported by the general classroom and school social climate' (McLaughlin et al 2010a, p.42). Indeed, some practitioners from local authorities had some concerns about certain schools' belief sets about pupils with SEN and/or disabilities (for example, whereby pupils with ASD are deemed as challenging and needing to be 'fixed', rather than the problem being located in other pupils' reactions).

As a result, these interventions were seen to run the risk of offering only short- to medium-term solutions to bullying behaviour, which could falter if not reinforced through a whole-school or community ethos. There is the possibility that, while they deal with an isolated event, they may not provide measures to stop the bullying happening again by other people at other times. This speaks to the wider problem of ensuring that a whole-school approach is fully embedded, particularly if these strategies also extend out into the community for lifetime and family-based work. They may also have significant resource implications, being dependent on funding from sources such as community services. Particularly in the current climate, these services are vulnerable to cuts.

Practitioners also reported that effective project work required intensive time and personal commitment to ensure that young people were supported and safe throughout the process. For example, Saylor and Leach's (2009) previously mentioned account of the Peer EXPRESS scheme required students' weekly participation in activities over a 24–27 week period. There were concerns that the peer group approaches may be seen as offering a 'quick-fix' over a small number of sessions, but that this is often not appropriate for children with SEN and/or disabilities. These young people may not respond to short periods of activity and may instead require several sessions to gain trust. This reinforces wider research which suggests that the duration and intensity of programmes are important factors in leading to decreases in bullying in general; as Farrington and Ttofi (2009, p.70) suggest, programmes need to be intensive and long-lasting to have an impact on this troubling problem. It could be that considerable time is needed in order to build up an appropriate school ethos that efficiently tackles bullying.

This conclusion is equally true for the use of awareness-raising project work, for which there are similar questions about the duration and extent of effects, given that they are time-limited and specific only to the particular individuals involved. They may lead to the creation of sustained relationships which can create a protective peer group – a known factor in protecting individuals against bullying – but as Farringdon and Ttofi intimate, this cannot be assumed and may not always be the case.

Category D: Approaches that empower and equip the individual to address bullying

Intervention 7: Individualised support and counselling

This intervention involved teachers and other practitioners working with children on a one-to-one basis, in order to both understand the factors and triggers that create bullying and to offer tailored advice on how to respond to bullying. The strategy used in Case study 7 involved the use of counsellors in secondary schools having confidential discussions about bullying. In other cases, it involved the use of specialist teachers in primary schools conducting one-to-one 'talk time' with individual children using metaphor, sand-tray play and puppets as ways of encouraging affected children to discuss and resolve bullying incidents in a safe environment. Most of this work was provided within schools, although there was one case of a local authority team providing one-to-one casework with individuals. Other variations included wider work with students with SEN and/ or disabilities to raise confidence, such as the design of a personalised curriculum and support via learning support staff.

Case study 7: Wroxham School

Wroxham School is a special school with around 240 pupils. They use a 'whole-school individualised approach', using mentoring in addition to other initiatives such as circle time, restorative justice approaches and quiet clubs. The individualised approach ensures that teachers know the children very well and respond to their specific individual needs, which they suggest is particularly important when dealing with children with SEN and/or disabilities.

An example of how this approach is employed in a bullying context is a situation where a child with ASD lashed out in the playground. A mentor was called, who removed the child from the situation. They sat in the school's book bus, and the boy was given a clipboard and asked to observe all the other children while the mentor gently unpicked what had happened. This enabled the child to feel contained, safe and in control. From the individualised counselling, it became apparent that this child needed certain toys to make playtimes easier, which was then acted upon. An incident form was completed and shared with all the people working with the child, from the headteacher to lunchtime supervisors.

This approach enables everyone to learn from specific incidents, understand the perspective of some of the school's more vulnerable students and respond with appropriate changes (in another occasion, monitoring of the lunchtime incident forms led to the setting up of a quiet club). The school claims low levels of bullying and cites positive feedback from parents and carers, teachers and lunchtime supervisors as further evidence of effectiveness.

Intervention 8: Confidence raising and skills training

The final, but no less important, intervention raised by practitioners was in the area of communication skills. These strategies aimed to raise students' confidence and resilience, equipping them with strategies and coping skills for going out in the community, gaining confidence in communicating and in maintaining friendships. They also involved children being taught specific skills that enabled them to deflect bullying, including the use of fogging techniques (that is, responding positively to name-calling), assertiveness skills and body-language awareness.

Case study 8: Changing Faces

Changing Faces is a voluntary organisation aimed at supporting young people with facial disfigurement. Among its responses to bullying is to teach children 'fogging' techniques (non-aggressive fielding of attitudes) and other special social skills. Individuals learn a range of practices to deal with fielding curiosity, staring, rude comments and verbal bullying. Other strategies address body language and teach positive self-talk. These training sessions are often used in transitions groups over the summer vacation to prepare children for attendance at secondary schools.

Changing Faces attempts to evaluate its work through individual feedback: measuring the confidence and skills of children before and after intervention. They report that these showed that, after a term, children's experiences of bullying were halved. Feedback from the young people who had worked in this way also suggests that, because it is fun and interesting, everyone involved feels more confident and competent. However, these strategies may rely on young people having adequate speech and language skills, which many children with SEN and/or disabilities do not have.

Effectiveness of approaches that equip the individual

The approaches presented here are distinctive in that they build up an individual's competence to respond to bullying more effectively themselves. Skills training approaches are deemed an important preventative strategy in stopping children with SEN from 'allowing' things happen to them; while individualised approaches (such as counselling and mentoring) provide children affected with important sources of support when the bullying actually occurs, through sympathetic adult help.

Practitioners raised positive feedback from parents and carers as evidence of the effectiveness of individualised support. An anecdote from teachers in one school showed that, following the introduction of this type of support, children who had previously avoided coming to school because of bullying were now attending. Social skills and communication techniques were seen as important in equipping children with lifelong skills, in contrast to other approaches which may be seen rather as 'emergency sticking plasters' applied when bullying incidents occur, which though effective in the short term, do not provide measures to stop the bullying occurring at other times, by other people. In contrast, equipping young people with techniques and appropriate responses was seen to give them confidence to address bullying whenever they occur in their lifetime. Such classes also address deeper rooted problems associated with bullying, such as the avoidance of challenging situations and the reluctance and limited skills of some children with SEN and/or disabilities to instigate friendships. Conversely, if done with students who are also bullies themselves, the lifetime skills learned may contribute to a more long-term decrease in anti-social behaviour. This is particularly important given that school bullying is 'an important risk marker of a more general anti-social development' (Bender and Lösel 2011, p.105).

However, some problems remain with both approaches. One difficulty of individualised initiatives is that they often rely on the willingness of children to disclose that there is a problem. However, it is known that many children do not always take this step for fear of retribution and further victimisation. Furthermore, there is a risk that isolating the children via one-to-one help with an adult may mark children with SEN and/or disabilities out as 'special' and increase the risk of stigmatisation. This is important to consider, given that the research shows that spending a lot of time with staff is itself something that can render individuals vulnerable to bullying (Chapter 1). There are also implications for staff, requiring significant time commitment. This can be mollified if all staff are committed to individualised attention as part of a whole-school ethos, but may place an untenable burden on few personnel identified as responsible for bullying and/or SEN if this is not the case. Where therapy approaches are used, there are also significant cost implications, which only schools with adequate scale can support, as they require staff to be adequately trained and receive ongoing supervision. The same resource implications are faced by schools offering skills training approaches, as to be effective, a student requires ongoing support over a number of sessions. A further difficulty with this approach is that the practices require competent and confident verbal communication, which many children with SEN and/or disabilities do not possess. There is also a danger that if managed poorly, it could exacerbate a bullying situation. Moreover, it places responsibility on the individual involved rather than on others to adapt their behaviours.

What can we conclude about effective practice to tackle bullying and SEN and/or disabilities?

There is undoubtedly a great deal of lively and interesting practice that is being carried out in schools and related bodies to respond to bullying among young people with SEN and/or disabilities. Discussions among practitioners demonstrated in-depth knowledge about where these had worked, and how they could be used in a variety of different complementary ways to address the problem. Coming together as a group of skilled individuals and listening to each other's practice through this exercise provided a further occasion for practitioners to validate their own practice, inviting informed listeners to probe interventions further and consider their effectiveness.

To able to move forward and offer a more systematic and evidenced guidance to other schools on which practice works, it was also clear that practitioners were limited by restrictions in the types of evidence that they could access to support their theories. Most participants were reflexive about this matter, and aware that there was little evidence-based evaluation of whether their practices were effective, with many relying on anecdotal and personal experience of what works. Self-evaluations for some of the interventions employed raised comments such as: 'the weakness in terms of evidence-based evaluation' and that 'measuring [the intervention's] impact is not embedded'. While this does not mean that the approaches are not effective, it does suggest that practitioners are not certain of methods or approaches to demonstrate that this is indeed so.

In terms of data offered to demonstrate effectiveness, monitoring processes were the only form that actually gave a detailed picture across schools of where, when and what type of bullying occurs, and also provided a baseline through which to compare trends year-on-year. However, apart from the example of East Sussex (see Case study 2), in practice it did not yet seem to be directed at assessing the efficacy of any of the other programmes identified. Where this *is* done, monitoring activity can be useful to help inform and direct practice: at East Sussex, monitoring data revealed that their existing approach to tackling bullying was not working well enough with the pupils with SEN and/or disabilities. Having noted this, they secured funding and developed a more accessible anti-bullying toolkit specifically for use with children with SEN and/or disabilities.

A great deal of evidence around effectiveness was subjective, personal opinion gained, for example, through evaluations of training days. Yet the teachers themselves often spoke passionately and enthusiastically about their approach, with most teachers convinced that their practice had real results. There was no shortage of 'soft' forms of validation, such as anecdotal accounts of behaviour improvement and lesser incidences of conflicts in classrooms. Others just had the 'feeling' that these strategies worked. While these must not be dismissed, it supports the observations by Farrington and Ttofi (2009, p.10), in their review of school-based programmes to reduce bullying and victimisation, that:

> *Many programs seem to have been based on common sense ideas about what might reduce bullying rather than on empirically-supported theories of why children bully, why children become victims, or why bullying events occur.*
> (Farrington and Ttofi 2009, p.10)

This raises interesting questions about the potential role of teachers in generating educational knowledge through teacher research and enquiry; and how they can turn their common-sense theories into new validated public knowledge (McIntyre 2008).

One interesting departure from this was the use of pre- and post-intervention surveys or scales, used particularly for evaluating the group approaches (Intervention 5). These were particularly important tools in assessing whether bullying had decreased, chiefly because they relied entirely on the perspectives of young people themselves rather than teachers' impressions of their effectiveness. This was also the case in examples of action research in our sample, where schools found often quite simple solutions through listening to the fears and difficulties of children. Even in these approaches, however, there is no way of knowing whether effectiveness was sustained over time in long-term reduction of bullying.

Conclusions

This chapter raises several questions, both based around what currently *is* as well as what *might be*. In conclusion, we suggest several implications: first, considering policy and practice; second, considering how more effective and evidence-based responses might be drawn; and finally, questioning values because some of the interventions raised here pose questions that strike at the very heart of debates around inclusion in schools.

Considering policy and practice

The evidence on current practice presented by schools suggests a number of implications for policy and practice and recommendations to address gaps and omissions. These can be considered under four complementary categories that are often used to enable change: leadership; strategies and policies; systems; and training and support.

Leadership

- Advocated as integral to the success of many of the other interventions was the development of a whole-school ethos, coupled with empathy building among peers addressing the wider psychosocial contexts of the bullying of those with SEN and/or disabilities. However, this relies on adequate vision, leadership and commitment and the development of initiatives that go beyond a school's usual remit. It therefore has implications for resources. It also relies on a well-informed understanding of the particularity of working with the bullying of pupils with SEN and/or disabilities. Leadership strategies and approaches are crucial and need to be informed and well directed.

Strategies and policies

- Consultations or action research or both – with students and/ or teachers as researchers – were raised as important means of responding to pupils' concerns, with case studies suggesting that they can enact important changes in school environments and practices. However they must be both inclusive and linked with systems to turn recommendations into practice. In this regard, it is necessary for schools to further demonstrate how accessible the established mechanisms are, in reality, to students with SEN and/or disabilities.
- Individualised approaches come at some cost and inevitably raise issues around funding and resourcing. We found examples of local authorities who would like to apply an individualised model, such as that demonstrated by East Sussex (Case study 2), but just did not have the resources to do so.
- Minimisation of bullying by teachers is acknowledged as a known problem; however, from April 2010 schools are open to legal redress if they fail to comply with the demands of the Equality Act 2010 (see

Chapter 6). Careful attention must be paid to how bullying policies are modified to be appropriate to the needs of students with SEN and/or disabilities.

Systems

- Monitoring was raised as a means of gaining insight into the specific nature and frequency of bullying incidences. It enables practitioners to target resources where they are required and improve the effectiveness of anti-bullying provision. To date, not all anti-bullying teams monitor for specific instances of bullying of young people with SEN and/or disabilities because it is not prioritised.
- Monitoring around SEN and/or disabilities works best when done not for its own sake but when linked to direct adaptations of policy that actively challenge identity-based bullying.

Training and support

- More personalised and individualised approaches such as skills, communication and confidence training are vaunted by practitioners as effective for pupils with SEN and/or disabilities, both to deal with occurrences of bullying and to diminish its likelihood.
- Skills and confidence training require specialised and ongoing support by adults, to minimise the risk of exacerbating bullying situations.
- Training and group work may be more effective when anti-bullying teams have the capacity to offer more individualised sessions over a longer time period, in order to accommodate and respond to a child's needs.
- More in-depth education of practitioners is required to address the barrier that some teachers have limited confidence in dealing with bullying if they perceive it as an individual failure to successfully manage relationships in their class or school.

The exercise shows that there are a variety of established and emerging practices, mostly in the arenas of approaches and strategies, systems and training, although leadership is perhaps the most crucial aspect in initiating change. The limited leadership evident thus far around this issue is indicative of a lack of maturity of the topic; but there were few participants who could confidently say that their approaches covered the whole spectrum, from leadership to training and support, and contained all the necessary elements of an effective anti-bullying approach tailored to children with SEN and/or disabilities.

How more effective and evidence-based responses might be drawn

If practitioners are committed to change, what should they be aspiring toward and how sure can they be that this is the correct path to take? Our research exposed a gap between theories of bullying and disability on the one hand and local practices on the other. It is vital that this gap between research and practice is bridged to ensure theory development is grounded in informed practice. The key to both is to establish a robust process and impact evaluation, one which provides a solid evidence base of demonstrably effective strategies to enable teachers and researchers to take account of its complexity and address this problem with confidence. At present, too little is known about the effects and outcomes to make firm conclusions about which are the 'most effective'.

Reflection is invited on the remit of schools; for instance, do they need to go further in taking responsibility for the wider social fabric and intervene in peer dynamics and interactions within the school? As Chapters 1 and 2 established, research suggests there might be scope, for instance, in cultivating positive attitudes to difference among pupils; promoting friendship; teaching social and communication skills; and in developing strategies for behaviours in non-teaching parts of the school day. It might also involve creating social opportunities for marginalised individuals to become more accepted by their peers. There may also be more to be done in detecting, monitoring and measuring bullying, particularly given that teachers tend to underestimate rates of this type of bullying. However, whichever strategy or combination of strategies is employed, it is vital that more effort is addressed at understanding – and confirming through systematic evaluations – why they work.

There are several reasons which complicate assessment of the current playing field. One is that this particular exercise exposed that many of the 'same' interventions are used differentially in different contexts, which makes it difficult to assess their efficacy in general. Certain approaches are found in very different settings, cultures and contexts, which potentially change the outcomes entirely. For example, the 'restorative justice' approach used in a 'zero tolerance' school context is vastly different to that found in another school with a non-punitive approach. While both schools use the same language, they may in fact be demonstrating quite different practice, which must be explored using robust process evaluation.

Questioning values

The concern exposed by this exercise speaks to the wider philosophies and values about inclusion in education. Many of the practices discussed in this chapter are simply existing anti-bullying strategies for *all* children. However, this makes it very difficult to pinpoint how far evaluations of 'success' relate to or differ from effectiveness specifically in relation to children with SEN and/or disabilities. Other interventions, by contrast, were focused entirely on children with SEN and/or disabilities (for example, nurture and transitions groups set these children apart from mainstream peers to offer targeted support). And, while the agenda for many years has been directed at minimising difference between children identified as having SEN and/or disabilities and others, some types of interventions positively evaluated in this exercise quite self-consciously bring attention to difference. For example, the awareness-raising projects draw attention to disabilities, by educating and informing other students about the implications of having a certain disability, much as former disability awareness programmes used to.

Some support emerges for the argument that general strategies used in anti-bullying programmes may need to be adapted for these young people. For example, group work based around a small number of sessions may have to be stretched over a longer duration for a child with SEN and/or disabilities to ensure that everything is fully understood. Indeed, it is refreshing to see East Sussex local authority's toolkit (Case study 2), which adapts its existing provision by providing printed materials and modifying the content of sessions on friendship for pupils with ASD, for example.

In order to develop approaches that we can have confidence in, we have developed a two-tiered typology for which interventions can – and also in the future, could be – judged (see Table 5.1).

Table 5.1: Typology for interventions

Basis of assessment of evidence	Level of approach
1. 'Hunch': feels good, common-sense assumption	1. Strategies for everyone
2. Anecdotal evidence: from teachers, parents and carers, and pupils	2. Strategies for some
3. Systematic data collection	3. Strategies for a few
4. Evidence that informs practice	4. Proactively SEN and/or disabilities specific

At present, most of the programmes that were encountered fall in the top half of this typology – being judged as effective because of common sense and anecdotal evidence. There are also differences in the degree to which they are specific to SEN. A more robust strategy for effectively responding to bullying that relates to young people with SEN and/or disabilities would involve the development of initiatives that fall at the bottom half of this typology, that is, those that are both evidence-based and SEN and/or disabilities specific. However, this requires a much firmer evidence base of practice. Although current research about interventions and their effectiveness is developing, 'there is still a need for much more research on school-based interventions and their efficacy' (McLaughlin et al 2010a, p.6).

Moreover, there is also a need to develop different warrants for the research on interventions; much of the research examined in the review was of university-based research, which has its own standards of rigour (for example, Chapters 1 and 2). A warrant for research on the school practices explored in this chapter is also required for practitioners to use and adapt themselves, in order to demonstrate the efficacy of their practice. This is important because ultimately, '[…] it is teachers who in practice determine the fate of proposed innovations, and whether or not they maintain the practices they have inherited, it is teachers who implicitly or explicitly evaluate the merits of different practices' (McLaughlin et al 2008, p.5).

Several recommendations emerge from the work with practitioners. There is a need for:

- local authorities, school leaders and other related organisations to develop an integrated approach which involves demonstrable leadership, policies, effective systems and targeted training and support
- a robust and comprehensive evaluation research programme to assess how effective different strategies are for young people with disabilities and to inform a more solution-supportive theory development
- the development of a warrant for research on practice that will be of value to practitioners and others working in this field.

6 Looking back and looking forward: Creating an agenda for the future

Colleen McLaughlin, Richard Byers, Caroline Oliver and Rosie Peppin-Vaughan

University of Cambridge Faculty of Education

This chapter draws out the main themes arising from the exploration of the different perspectives and so will look back on the early chapters. It also looks forward and draws out the implications of our work for future research and practice development in schools.

Looking back: what have we learned from this study?

It matters to all

First, and most importantly, we have learned that it is a serious issue, which deserves much more attention and resources. Young people spoke passionately about their experiences of being bullied, as did their parents and carers. There is a plea in these pages for this issue to be taken seriously by all those who work with young people and especially by those who work in schools. The research backs this up. Rates of bullying for young people with SEN and/or disability are unacceptably high. There is a great weight of evidence that confirms that young people with SEN and/or disabilities are significantly more likely to be bullied or victimised than their non-disabled peers. Further, these rates of vulnerability to bullying for young people with SEN and/or disabilities are very significant. The young people consulted talked of it as being an almost permanent feature of their interpersonal landscape. This must change, as it has for many other young people who have experienced a shift in understanding and policy on bullying. Issues of difference, visibility and need are central to being bullied: so, too, is the need for us to focus on the acceptance of difference. This is not easy but it is worthwhile.

Second, we have had confirmation of the long-term and pernicious consequences of bullying. The Equality and Human Rights Commission (2011) and others have articulated very clearly how important and under-examined this issue is; and how necessary it is to take this bullying very seriously indeed. It can be viewed as a continuum, which begins with bullying at school and can culminate in some of the very serious incidents examined within the EHRC inquiry. Pupils with SEN and/or disabilities tend to be less accepted and more rejected by their peers than other children, even when they have studied within a stable peer group for a number of years. Poor peer acceptance is known to lead to a greater risk of victimisation and bullying. Some reports indicate that these problems get worse as young people grow older and move into secondary schools. Furthermore, children with comorbid conditions (combinations of difficulties) report higher levels of peer victimisation. Teasing and bullying are reported to be additive, meaning that the chances of being bullied are compounded for children with combinations of difficulties or characteristics of 'difference'. Further, being bullied can, in itself, increase vulnerability to further bullying. For some young people, this cycle leads to extreme violence and hate crime.

Understanding the dynamic

The research has given us a much greater understanding of the processes of bullying, so helping us to think further about interventions. It shows that bullying is a social process related to social competence and social opportunity. It shows the dynamics of bullying. Young people with SEN and/or disabilities have many characteristics that make them vulnerable to bullying, including lower academic attainment, physical differences, shyness and passivity, low self-esteem and anxiety, and behaviour that challenges other people. Some young people become involved in teasing and bullying as well as being bullied themselves, arguably because they have difficulty monitoring and controlling their behaviour in social situations. There is also some evidence that young people who are rejected may be more likely to respond by adopting bullying behaviours. The research strongly suggests that the key determinants of vulnerability to bullying are associated with language, communication, social skills and status. This is because dialogue is generally the medium through which young people initiate contact, exchange information and negotiate shared roles. Young people with SEN and/or disabilities frequently experience difficulties in language and communication. Young people in the mainstream of education tend to have good 'discourse awareness' and to be skilled at detecting strengths and weaknesses in conversation. They may define social competence according to linguistic competence and respond accordingly, so that poor language skills (and particularly poor receptive language skills) become a predictor of peer rejection.

Social behaviours are crucially important with regard to peer victimisation. Young people with SEN and/or disabilities are often described in the research as being at risk of being bullied because of their 'low social ability', 'deficits in decoding social situations', 'reduced social competence', or 'impaired social tendencies'. There is wide agreement that social issues, related to peer rejection, are key factors in the bullying of young people with SEN and/or disabilities. It may relate to language and communication issues and to the difficulties that some young people may experience in interpreting non-verbal cues, communication messages and the feelings associated with those messages. Communication problems and the misinterpretation of social situations may be key elements leading to an increased risk of being bullied. Social isolation and victimisation can lead to further exacerbated victimisation in an ongoing cycle of bullying and rejection.

This understanding of the social dynamics reinforces the need for the development and support of social agency amongst young people with SEN and/or disabilities. This will involve many things: devising interventions that promote understanding; shaping the social context of the school; providing social opportunity; working to enhance the positive impact of the peer group; and exerting as much influence as we can in a constructive fashion. Enhancing inclusion in the peer group should be an aim of our work. It will require organisational change as well as the construction of participative practices. This will be discussed in more detail later on.

Looking back at the research

We scrutinised the research for evidence relating to interventions and we also engaged with teachers and schools about the challenges they had and how they validated their practice. Despite good intentions, there is evidence that teachers tend to underestimate, undervalue or discount reports of bullying from pupils with SEN and/or disabilities.

There are also challenges in monitoring bullying and in accessing the views of the young people. The challenge is to find an appropriate and effective way of developing awareness so that teachers feel confident and comfortable about reporting incidents of bullying in their classes. This is crucial, as teachers are the adults who spend most time directly in contact with students. Relying solely on teacher or pupil reports can be problematic, since studies have shown that teachers often underestimate or have an inaccurate sense of levels of bullying; and students with SEN and/or disabilities may not recognise bullying situations, either as perpetrators or victims. Linked to this is the issue of defining bullying: it is important for schools to have a commonly agreed definition, shared by both teachers and pupils. This is especially important as members of both groups are known to have differing interpretations of the behaviours they observe in schools. Teachers in discussions about their practice also suggested that they wanted to monitor bullying as it affects young people with SEN and/or disabilities but needed tools and guidance on how to do this.

Social conditions of classrooms and schools: interventions that show promise

There were two areas of intervention: the preventative and the reactive. In our examination of the intervention studies, there were some rich veins to mine. There were examples of approaches in which the social conditions of the peer group and of the classroom had been impacted upon to the benefit of young people with SEN and/or disabilities. Interventions that engaged an empathic understanding of the complexity and nature of the social dynamic had an impact upon bullying. It would appear that not having a reason for, or a way of understanding, your peers' behaviour can be frightening and unhelpful for young people. These interventions need to be lead by professionals who understand the complexity and delicacy of the task; and the interventions need to be sustained and informed, not one-off events.

Working with peers is central to successfully intervening to change the dynamic, and there is still a need for more evidence on how this works.

The impact of forms of organisation and ways of treating young people with SEN and/or disability

It is also important not to adopt a solely individual perspective or a 'within child' explanation or lens. The contextual elements of the school and the classroom need to be examined. There is also evidence that the ways in which schooling for pupils with special educational needs and/or disabilities operates can exacerbate the problems young people face by requiring them to be passive and compliant; over-protecting them; providing them with inappropriate staff support; teaching them outside their peer group; failing to ensure equality of physical access to environments and activities; and requiring them to seek help because the work has not been adjusted in order to be accessible to them.

There is a need to examine the processes in the school that enhance or decrease difference or which engage with it in a positive or negative way. Contextual features, including staff support, poorly differentiated teaching and separate teaching, may mean that young people with SEN and/or disabilities do not have the right opportunities to forge protective links with their peers. Children who are not effectively integrated and who rely on staff support may become victims of bullying and teasing. This reinforces the need to develop agency amongst young people. It is the unstructured parts of the school day that can prove problematic: we need to help young people to cope with these and to give them support.

We cannot do this work alone and, although it may be a sensitive task, it is vital that young people with SEN and/or disability are involved in describing the nature of the task and in shaping the response. This is in itself an activity that enhances agency. The views of the young people consulted for this study show how powerful and useful such a consultation can be.

Looking back at young people's views

What is striking when reading the views of the young people is to see the overlap with research findings and the maturity of the views expressed. First, and most importantly, they confirmed the powerful impact of being bullied and its omnipresence in their lives. The young people told of how the bullying they experienced often went unnoticed and unchallenged. They argued that it was how behaviour was seen by adults (often not seen as bullying or seen as acceptable) that was key. They also saw it as essentially about difference and how difference is treated. Again confirming research findings, they argued that schools could impact upon the attitudes to, and behaviour around, difference and its tolerance or intolerance. Their own understandings of difference varied greatly and appeared to be strongly linked to the ways in which individual schools framed this issue. The ethos of the school and the school's commitment to tackling bullying had a significant impact on young people's understanding of why bullying happens. All young people related the causes of bullying to 'difference' in some form or another. They also described their own fears of retaliation and of being disbelieved, exemplifying the complexity of the task of responding appropriately. However, they argued passionately for the right and for the need to be involved in giving their views on the nature of the bullying as well as on the responses to it. They wanted to be treated as partners in development. This joint engagement with the issues may well be the vehicle for addressing the complexity.

Non-punitive approaches

Despite the difficulties that they experienced, the young people, including some who experienced high levels of bullying, could empathise with the young person who had been bullying them and offered explanations as to why they thought this might happen. Many thought the young person who was bullying might also need help and support as, for example, they may have experienced bullying themselves or, due to their own impairment, may not understand that their behaviour would be perceived as bullying. They needed support to understand this. The notion of difference was not only evident in their understanding of why certain young people experience bullying, but also in their understanding of why young people might display bullying behaviours.

So there were clear messages from these young people about wanting to be fully involved in making change happen; about wanting adopted approaches to take account of their actual and lived experience of bullying; and about how they strongly supported and preferred a graduated, non-punitive or non-sanction-based response to bullying. They argued for an understanding and valuing of difference and disability as an effective way of preventing bullying occurring in the first place. They wanted responses to bullying that looked beyond the specific act or incident; responses that focused on enabling young people to understand each other and work to develop a friendship or mutually agreed solution. The young people with SEN and/or disability believed strongly that if other young people were supported to understand and value difference and disability, then this would be an effective way to prevent 'disablist' bullying. They discussed interventions and thought that effective prevention strategies might include disability awareness and equality training; lessons for pupils, teachers and support staff; positive images of disability within the school setting; and the positive portrayal of disability throughout the school curriculum. Finally, they wanted help in shaping their response and understanding too. These strategies were seen as helpful in the intervention studies we reviewed, so there is much support for their adoption.

Looking back at the family perspective

The cruelty of some of the incidents is stark in the accounts from the families. The impact on all, and the severity of the incidents stands out.

What also emerges is the emotional complexity of dealing with an incident of bullying. For the child concerned it is complex, both to disclose and to contemplate action being taken. There is an understandable fear of the consequences. So finding out is not necessarily straightforward.

In the eyes of parents and carers, the response from the school was not satisfactory in the majority of cases (68 per cent of those who responded felt unhappy with the outcome). A punitive response may result in the wrong person being punished, and some cases of this were reported. The dynamic nature of bullying emerges again as a theme, alongside the need to engage with it as a process and not necessarily as a simple event. Interventions that were seen as helpful were similar to those viewed as helpful by young people and reinforced by research findings: for example, specific direct action, fostering understanding and peer approaches. Unhelpful responses included denying the incident was one of bullying or downplaying the severity of it. When a young person was punished for retaliating, this was seen as highly unjust. There were some indications that some parents and carers wanted more of a punitive approach. Good communication is a major theme, as is the need for professionals to keep communicating at all stages of the processes.

Looking forward: the agenda for the future

The evidence from multiple perspectives raised by this book is compelling. It is vital that the messages are acted upon quickly to ensure a different landscape in our schools for children growing up with SEN and/or disabilities. What would that alternative look like and how do we get there?

In this final section, in addition to conclusions drawn from the research studies and consultations, we draw on the reflections on our findings that were offered by experts and practitioners and aim to set an agenda for the future to eliminate the problem of bullying for these children. The suggestions were given at two events, which we recorded. The first was the conference held at Cambridge University in autumn 2010 (see Appendix 1 for the methodology) where, in the final stage of the event, participants were invited to consider these questions:

- What do you consider should be the developments in practice and school policy? What should have priority?
- How does this compare with current practice?
- How do you think the practice could and should be validated?

The second event was the 'practice dialogue event', jointly presented in London by National Children's Bureau, the Anti-Bullying Alliance, Council for Disabled Children, and University of Cambridge Faculty of Education, in Spring 2011. This is where each of the component parts of the project were brought together. Professionals from a variety of policy and practice backgrounds reflected on the implications of the project and set out their positions on what should happen next in relation to research, practice, policy and wider dissemination of the findings.

An agenda for research

A future agenda must prioritise further research and it should focus on joint practice development with researchers and practitioners working together. We have identified fruitful subjects for exploration and also some indications of the type of research needed, which should aim to inform, develop and study practice development.

The reason why research should have such a high priority on any future agenda is because it was recognised that, while some schools do currently have some suitable responses they are unable to show that their interventions are effective and efficient in addressing this type of bullying. Many practitioners felt rather lacking in direction and very keen to have more guidance. Practitioners wanted to have more access to the existing evidence base in this area, in order to inform their policy and practice development. There is a clear appetite for monitoring and reviewing the effectiveness of approaches to identify successes. Although practitioners were cognisant that there was no 'one approach to tackle bullying', they saw research as the way to identify promising approaches and develop well-defined responses, with clear measures of impact. There has not been any research in the UK similar to the Sheffield study of the development of approaches to bullying in schools. There is now sufficient evidence to show the need to have a similar approach to working with the bullying of pupils with SEN and/or disability, as this is a complex territory requiring more than the approaches developed in more general anti-bullying work. There is much research on different aspects but there is a need to be more holistic in the development and in the research.

The areas of development and research are also clearer: they relate to engagement with the social dimensions of schooling, including developing language and communication skills. The development of social agency, social opportunity and social competence in young people with SEN and/or disability has been established as a key focus. This will involve the development of work within peer groups, classrooms and schools. It will involve implementing collaborative and participatory pedagogies as well as examining the social contexts in school. The social context is of crucial importance: social competence with peers is a key factor in protecting pupils from bullying and victimisation. Pupils who are isolated from their peer group (for example, through separate teaching arrangements or by the constant presence of adult support) are at greater risk. The practitioners and policy-makers felt that social development among young people was an area of education that merited more attention than it is currently receiving. As well as the identification of bullying, other participants wanted researchers to explore the longer-term impacts of bullying for young people. Some felt that understanding how bullying affects life after school, and whether it had impacts on their lives afterwards, was important.

There was a need to develop a warrant for research-informed action. Practitioners do not have time to engage in lengthy projects and they were keen to know how to evaluate their actions. However, it is important not to underestimate the challenge this brings. On the one hand, it is unrealistic and possibly unproductive to impute externally defined formats of impact evaluation to schools as defined by academics or government departments. However, that does not mean we can simply revert to defining success in teacher terms, and ignore the fundamentals of robust and objective evaluation. The answer potentially lies in developing an action-oriented evaluation design that allows teachers to influence the aims and participate in data gathering, whilst professional researchers develop the appropriate methods; oversee their application; and guarantee robust analysis for joint interpretation, conclusions and recommendations. Social research methodology has evolved greatly over the last three decades, recognising and valuing multiple perspectives to inform and enrich an inspiring evaluation that should allow the identification of promising approaches and improve practice whilst starting to map the determining factors. There is a paucity of detailed qualitative studies of the complexity of practice in schools relating to the bullying of pupils with SEN and/or disability.

An agenda for practice

There are certain key arenas for the development of practice: curriculum, policy and ethos; students' roles and perspectives; practitioner training; and monitoring.

Curriculum, policy and ethos

Both researchers and practitioners in discussion advocated the need for attention to the social domain and particularly the development of social competence. It was argued that a stronger attention to social skills (both for pupils with and without SEN and/or disabilities) needed to be embedded throughout the formal and informal curriculum as a hopeful path to achieve inclusion and equality. On one hand, this could be through working with young people with SEN and/or disabilities, empowering them with language skills and more confidence. On the other hand, this problem could be addressed through developing inclusive practices for everyone and, by so doing, enable pupils with SEN and/or disabilities to be seen to be valuable and positive members of the school community. While it was recognised that recent drives to ensure 'every child matters' had some purchase among teaching staff, this message needed to be embedded among the pupil body more effectively, with more positive strategies for empathy building and teaching altruism. Indeed, it was felt that there was a lot of work to be done on empathy and making sure that it was developed throughout the whole curriculum. Some discussion was held about the status of the 'anti-bullying' message in schools, with some in favour of it being packaged in such a way that it was presented as being about understanding difference and developing equal expectations for all. Such a broadly inclusive and skills-focused approach might also involve identifying and showcasing the skills of pupils identified with SEN and/or disabilities. As one participant suggested:

> Is it just teaching each other to get to know each other so that differences are normalised and people aren't so solidly located in their nominal categories separately?

Students' roles and perspectives

The engagement of students in assessment and in the development of practice emerges in many ways in *Perspectives on Bullying and Difference*. The pupils themselves argue strongly for it and emerge as sophisticated analysers of both the problem and approaches to it. This provoked discussion of how far 'bullying' should be addressed head on, for example, by explicitly labelling and responding to a behaviour as 'bullying', or through equipping students with the social skills to manage and address 'difference'. In some quarters, it was suggested that perhaps the word 'bullying' gets in the way of effective resolution. Such considerations relate to a broader issue of how actions and behaviours perceived by adults as 'bullying' may be evaluated differently by peers, particularly in cases where children have disabilities involving social difficulties, and 'bullying' involves a manifestation of a cumulative set of misunderstandings. More attention could be paid to developing a shared language and definitions of concepts. This may also provide the groundwork for more effective solutions, given that most students seek reconciliation rather than punishment, and still seek to be socially on a good footing with classmates, even if they have been their victim.

In particular, practitioners also spoke of the need to develop more student ownership of bullying policies and procedures through a bottom-up approach in which the views of students are taken more seriously. This could be implemented easily through 'student voice' initiatives (with careful attention to how reflective they are of vulnerable students' perspectives); pupil surveys, using students as researchers on the topic; or through allowing more dialogue and opportunities to share experiences. However, as one participant pointed out, in consulting pupils to ensure that judgements about anti-bullying are more effective, one only gets a response as good as the questions that are asked. It was emphasised that communications therefore need to be addressed using the pupils' understandings. An example suggested as part of a 'bullying audit' aimed at giving a general picture of bullying in a school would be the question: What's fair and unfair about the practices at this school?

Certainly a strong message emerging for a future agenda is about how practitioners might respond more effectively to the voices of children. A particular concern is the onus on adults to be receptive in hearing difficult messages: some suggested that further attention might be directed at enabling teachers to 'hear what is hard to hear'. Particularly when dealing with such an emotive topic, in which bullying is a stigma, it is imperative to break down the knee-jerk response to do nothing because it is easier to do so, and replace this with honest and frank communication. Given that responsiveness to students was an area for further development, some suggestions were also around working with practitioners to act *promptly* and *visibly* to what children say. The research suggested that too many young people were being made to wait and not given any finality, and an alternative was the development of a positive timeline with the actions of multiple agencies recorded. Christine Lenehan, director of the Council for

Disabled Children, said at the practice dialogue event that 'the worst thing that you deal with all the time is an attitude that says it doesn't matter'.

Practitioners felt that some of the strategies prompted attention to the ways that teachers and support staff conceptualised children with SEN and/ or disabilities. It was felt that a balance must be struck between giving support and encouraging independence in students. In particular, it was noted that some children with SEN and/or disabilities are at risk of being 'overly protected and therefore isolated from the peer interactions that might actually be serving them better in school as well as out of school'. This requires attention to the role of adults starting from early years, with the awareness that if dependency is created at nursery stage, it is difficult to break that cycle further on in a child's school career. Further attention was therefore urged for school management to look at the role of auxiliary staff in supporting young people.

Practitioner training

Further training of practitioners was also raised as a future priority. There was a need for simple information-provision to raise awareness and spread the message but there was also a need for 'educating the educators' in this area, as teachers are lacking confidence in both recognising the issues and knowing what to do when confronted with bullying of this nature. This relates back to the need for robust validation of work in this area. The general poverty of training around this issue was mentioned. Some suggested that training would focus on generalising skills so that teachers can support interventions at classroom level, and another suggestion was that forums of good practice should be established.

Training may equally require focusing on staff attitudes or working with practitioners to enable them to hear some of the difficult messages associated with this topic (as discussed above). This was felt to be important to address even for managers, who, as a participant suggested 'need to be trained to notice the subtleties of bullying'. It was also suggested that training was not a cure alone, but required corresponding commitment to interventions, which must therefore be written into school development and CPD (continuing professional development) plans. This may require the nomination of designated lead professionals within schools who have the time and resources to implement initiatives and evaluate progress in relation to this topic.

Monitoring

A final theme, which was vigorously tabled, was the need to have a clear picture of the current state of play within schools and the ability to extract objective data on how the situation changes over time. Suggestions included the development of a bullying audit, as well as rigorous recording of bullying episodes for identified vulnerable groups, and the monitoring and evaluation of approaches to tackle the problem. Solution-focused scores for interventions were suggested to provide a measure of effectiveness, but there was also recognition that gaining a fair picture of what was really going on in a school around bullying meant careful attention to broader issues. This included teachers' observations of whether improvements had occurred, as well as broader issues such as pupil attendance and engagement. Discussion centred on why a picture of SEN-related bullying in schools does not already easily emerge, and why schools are currently not already recording this data. There was recognition that such processes were time-consuming and that this was evidently not prioritised when not only was there no accountability for achieving targets in this area but that nobody was asking for it. Such awareness leads us to the next level: policy.

An agenda for policy

Interest was sparked in what could be the drivers of this work to persuade headteachers that this is an area they should be addressing. Two key aspects of national policy were discussed: first, the Equalities Act; and second, Ofsted. The Equality Act 2010 recognises the impact of, for example, homophobic or disablist bullying and defines it as a form of harassment. The draft code of practice on schools, for example, includes no less than four explicit references to bullying, making very clear that disablist bullying is an unlawful act with potential for legal recourse. However, some participants wanted to go further and posited that disablist bullying should be conceived of as a hate crime. This issue is likely to gain momentum with the publication of the Equality and Human Rights Commission's Disability Harassment Inquiry (EHRC, 2011), which looks at disability harassment across British society. If anything, the inquiry report leaves no doubt as to the extremely harrowing consequences of what once started as bullying. For all those reasons, it was suggested that there needs to be a systematic approach to monitoring of what is happening, with a clearer balance established between safeguarding and equalities.

In relation to Ofsted, it was suggested that the findings of this research exercise should be taken into account when revising the standards expected of schools. Attention to what schools are doing to identify and adequately respond to this form of bullying should be an issue with the new 'behaviour and safety' track of the Ofsted inspection. Inspectors should also be trained in awareness of some of the strategies used to tackle the issue.

Behind these mechanisms, the message can also be reinforced by the well-being agenda. In this regard, there were also some cost–benefit arguments to be made in terms of the links that could be made with future health and well-being boards. In other words, given that GPs and GP consortia would likely be picking up children affected by this problem under mental health and well-being (and arguably the police force also in responding to potential longer term or extra-school problems), it was suggested that there was further scope in getting whole communities to recognise their responsibilities in this area.

However, there was concern in some quarters that there are tensions between the well-being and the attainment agendas in schools, with the former holding lesser importance than it once did. Moreover there was a very real risk that, with the current spate of ongoing transitions and restructuring, educational support services were losing practitioners with key skills in this area.

An agenda for dissemination

It was felt that the issue of disablist bullying required greater public awareness. This was at multiple levels. For instance in schools, it was felt that this form of bullying required a much higher profile. Other types of difference, such as race or gender, were felt to be well publicised, and to have been established as areas requiring care, attention and effective prioritisation. One participant demonstrated this by comparing the immediate response to racist bullying with a typical response to bullying among children with SEN and/or disabilities.

> it's stamped on immediately and [...] teachers jump all over it and they recognise it and they know that they must act. Whereas [...] teachers feeling that name-calling of children with disabilities is just kind of teasing and you know, not particularly serious and you don't quite understand the profound effect it can have.

In this respect, it was important to construct a coherent response to this work and make sure the message is received by school practitioners of the need and urgency to be alert to this issue. Equally important was the delivery of this message, via the key drivers (identified in the policy agenda above), to ensure that the message is not delivered in silos and as a one-off message.

There was also a feeling that the issues required a concerted public awareness campaign related to the findings of the research, disseminated via the media and through education, to mobilise parents and young people themselves. It was felt that this might involve getting celebrities involved and using MPs, to make sure that everybody is aware of this particular issue.

One suggestion emerging from the notion of public campaigning was to ensure that the message of this research goes out to schools through ongoing Anti-Bullying Week activities. These were felt to offer opportunities to raise awareness but also to begin to develop some practical responses. In summing up the responses from participants, it is pleasing to be able to report that *Perspectives on Bullying and Difference* comes partly as a means of fulfilling a small part of that aim.

Summary

It is clear that the future agenda will need to entail action and reflection – in research, practice, policy and communication – if it is to be effective. There is a need to engage with the complexity of the issue, in both research and practice, and that is not an easy task. Reducing the research or fragmenting the agenda will not help, as the research and discussions have shown. This agenda therefore needs passion as well as endurance in the short, medium and long term to make a real difference. The topic of working with difference, and finding constructive strategies for managing young people's responses to difference, has become a central concern for education and research.

References

Alderson, P and Goodey, C (1999) 'Autism in special and inclusive schools: "There has to be a point to their being there"', *Disability and Society*, 14, 2, 249–61.

Atlas, RS, Rona, S and Pepler, DJ (1998) 'Observations of bullying in the classroom', *Journal of Educational Research*, 92, 86–99.

Attwood, T (2004) 'Strategies to reduce the bullying of young children with Asperger syndrome', *Australian Journal of Early Childhood*, 29, 3, 15–23.

Baker, ET, Wang, MC and Walberg, HJ (1994–5) 'The effects of inclusion on learning', *Educational Leadership*, 52, 4, 33–5.

Baumeister, AL, Storch, EA and Geffken, GR (2008) 'Peer victimization in children with learning disabilities', *Child and Adolescent Social Work Journal*, 25, 1, 11–23.

Bauminger, N, Edelstein, HS and Morash, J (2005) 'Social information processing and emotional understanding among children with LD', *Journal of Learning Disabilities*, 38, 1, 45–61.

Bejerot, S and Mortberg, E (2009) 'Do autistic traits play a role in the bullying of obsessive-compulsive disorder and social phobia sufferers?', *Psychopathology*, 42, 3, 170–6.

Bender, D and Lösel, F (2011) 'Bullying at school as a predictor of delinquency, violence and other anti-social behavior in adulthood', *Criminal Behaviour and Mental Health*, 21, 99–106.

Besag, V (1989) *Bullies and Victims in Schools: A guide to understanding and management.* Milton Keynes: Open University Press.

Botting, N and Conti-Ramsden, G (2000) 'Social and behavioural difficulties in children with language impairment', *Child Language Teaching and Therapy*, 16, 2, 105–20.

Bromfield, R, Weisz, JR and Messer, T (1986) 'Children's judgments and attributions in response to the "mentally retarded" label: A developmental approach', *Journal of Abnormal Psychology*, 95, 1, 81–7.

Byers, R et al (2008) *What About Us? Promoting emotional well-being and inclusion by working with young people with learning difficulties in schools and colleges* (final report). London/Cambridge: Foundation for People with Learning Disabilities/ University of Cambridge Faculty of Education.

Campbell, JM (2006) 'Changing children's attitudes toward autism: A process of persuasive communication', *Journal of Developmental and Physical Disabilities*, 18, 251–72.

Campbell, JM (2007) 'Middle-school students' response to the self-introduction of a student with autism: Effects of perceived similarity, prior awareness, and educational message', *Remedial and Special Education*, 28, 163–73.

Carter, BB and Spencer, VG (2006) 'The fear factor: Bullying and students with disabilities', *International Journal of Special Education*, 21, 1, 11–23.

Cavallaro, SA and Porter, RH (1980) 'Peer preferences of at-risk and normally developing children in preschool mainstream classrooms', *American Journal of Mental Deficiency*, 84, 357–66.

Chazan, M, Laing, AF and Davies, D (1994) *Emotional and Behavioural Difficulties in Middle Childhood: Identification, assessment and intervention in school*. London: Falmer Press.

Children Act 1989: Local authority provision of services for children in need and their families. London: HMSO.

Coie, JD and Cillessen, AHN (1993) 'Peer rejection: Origins and effects on children's development', *Current Directions in Psychological Science*, 2, 3, 89–92.

Contact a Family (2010) *A Guide to Dealing with Bullying: For parents with disabled children*. London: Contact a Family.

DCSF (Department for Children, Schools and Families) (2007) *Social and Emotional Aspects of Learning for Secondary Schools*. London: DCSF.

DCSF (Department for Children, Schools and Families) (2008a) *Bullying Involving Children with Special Educational Needs and Disabilities: Safe to learn – embedding anti-bullying work in schools*. London: DCSF.

DCSF (Department for Children, Schools and Families) (2008b) *Preventing and Responding to Homophobic Bullying in Schools*. London: DCSF.

DfES (Department for Education and Skills) (2000) *Don't Suffer in Silence: An anti-bullying pack for schools*. London. DfES.

de Monchy, M, Pijl, SJ and Zandberg, T (2004) 'Discrepancies in judging social inclusion and bullying of pupils with behaviour problems', *European Journal of Special Needs Education*, 19, 3, 317–30.

Dickens, C (1854) *Hard Times*. London: Bradbury and Evans.

Didden, R et al (2009) 'Cyberbullying among students with intellectual and developmental disability in special education settings', *Developmental Neurorehabilitation*, 12, 3, 146–51.

Disability Discrimination Act 2005. London: HMSO.

Dixon, R (2006) 'A framework for managing bullying that involves students who are deaf or hearing impaired', *Deafness and Education International*, 8, 1, 11–32.

Dixon, R, Smith, P and Jenks, C (2004) 'Bullying and difference: A case study of peer group dynamics in one school', *Journal of School Violence*, 3, 4, 41–58.

Dockrell, J and Lyndsay, G (2000) 'Meeting the needs of children with specific speech and language difficulties', *European Journal of Special Needs Education*, 15, 1, 24–41.

East Sussex Anti-bullying Team (2010) *A Practitioner's Toolkit: Responding to bullying of children and young people with special educational needs and disabilities*. East Sussex County Council.

Elam, JJ and Sigelman, CK (1983) 'Developmental differences in reactions to children labeled mentally retarded', *Journal of Applied Developmental Psychology*, 4, 303–15.

Equality and Human Rights Commission (EHRC) (2011) *Hidden in Plain Sight: Inquiry into disability-related harassment*. London: EHRC [available online at www.equalityhumanrights.com/dhfi].

Erhardt, D and Hinshaw, SP (1994) 'Initial sociometric impressions of attention-deficit hyperactivity disorder and comparison boys: Predictions from social behaviors and from nonbehavioral variables', *Journal of Consulting and Clinical Psychology*, 62, 4, 833–42.

Etherington, A (2007) 'Bullying and teasing and helping children with ADS: What can we do?', *Good Autism Practice*, 8, 2, 37–44.

Equality Act 2010, s15. London: HMSO.

European Agency for Development in Special Needs Education (ed CJW Meijer) (2003) *Special Education across Europe in 2003: Trends in provision in 18 European countries*. Middelfart, Denmark: European Agency for Development in Special Needs Education.

Faris, R and Felmlee, D (2011) 'Status struggles: Network centrality and gender segregation in same- and cross-gender aggression', *American Sociological Review*, 76, 1, 48–73.

Farmer, TW (1993) 'Misconceptions of peer rejection and problem behaviour: Understanding aggression in students with mild disabilities', *Remedial and Special Education*, 21, 4, 194–208.

Farrington, DP (1993) 'Understanding and preventing bullying', *Crime and Justice*, 17, 381–458.

Farrington, DP and Ttofi, MM (2009) *School-based Programs to Reduce Bullying and Victimisation*. Oslo: Campbell Systematic Reviews.

Fox, CL and Bolton, MJ (2005) 'The social skills problems of victims of bullying: Self, peer and teacher perceptions', *British Journal of Educational Psychology*, 75, 2, 313–28.

Frederickson, N (2010) 'Bullying or befriending? Children's responses to classmates with special needs', *British Journal of Special Education*, 37, 1, 4–12.

Frederickson, N and Furnham, A (2004) 'The relationship between socio-metric status and peer-assessed behavioural characteristics of included pupils who have moderate learning difficulties and their classroom peers', *British Journal of Educational Psychology*, 74, 2, 391–410.

Frederickson, N et al (2007) 'Assessing the social and affective outcomes of inclusion', *British Journal of Special Education*, 34, 2, 105–15.

Geisthardt, C and Munsch, DG (1996) 'Coping with school stress: A comparison of adolescents with and without learning disabilities', *Journal of Learning Disabilities*, 29, 3, 287–96.

Gilmour, J and Skuse, D (1996) 'Short stature: The role of intelligence in psychosocial adjustment', *Archives of Diseases in Childhood*, 75, 25–31.

Goldman, LG (1987) 'Social implications of language disorder', *Journal of Reading, Writing and Learning Disabilities International*, 3, 119–30.

Gottlieb, J and Leyser, Y 'Friendships between mentally retarded and non-retarded children', in SR Asher and JM Gottman (eds)(1981) *The Development of Children's Friendships*. New York: Cambridge University Press.

Gottlieb, J, Semmel, M and Veldman, DJ (1978) 'Correlates of social status among mainstreamed mentally retarded children', *Journal of Educational Psychology*, 70, 396–405.

Greenham, S (1999) 'Learning disabilities and psychosocial adjustment: A critical review', *Child Neuropsychology*, 5, 3, 171–96.

Gresham, FM and MacMillan, DL (1997) 'Social competence and affective characteristics of students with mild disabilities', *Review of Educational Research*, 67, 377–415.

Guralnick, MJ 'The peer relations of younger handicapped and non-handicapped children', in PS Strain, MJ Guralnick and HM Walker (eds)(1986) *Children's Social Behaviour: Development, assessment and modification*. Orlando, Florida: Academic Press.

Hanish, LD and Guerra, NG (2000) 'Children who get victimized at school: What is known? What can be done?', *Professional School Counseling*, 4, 113–19.

Hargreaves, DH (2004) *Personalising Learning 2: Student voice and assessment for learning*. London: Specialist Schools Trust.

Hemphill, L and Siperstein, GN (1990) 'Conversational competence and peer response to mildly retarded children', *Journal of Educational Psychology*, 82, 1, 128–34.

Henderson, SE and Hall, D (1982) 'Concomitants of clumsiness in young school children', *Developmental Medicine and Child Neurology*, 24, 448–60.

Hodson, P, Baddeley, A and Laycock, S (2005) 'Helping secondary schools to be more inclusive of Year 7 pupils with SEN', *Educational Psychology in Practice*, 21, 1, 53–67.

Holmberg, K and Hjern, A (2008) 'Bullying and attention-deficit-hyperactivity disorder in 10-year-olds in a Swedish community', *Developmental Medicine and Child Neurology*, 50, 2, 134–8.

Holzbauer, JJ (2008) 'Disability harassment observed by teachers in special education', *Journal of Disability Policy Studies*, 19, 3, 162–71.

Hugh-Jones, S and Smith, PK (1999) 'Self-reports of short- and long-term effects of bullying on children who stammer', *British Journal of Educational Psychology*, 69, 2, 141–58.

Humphrey, JL, Storch, EA and Geffken, GR (2007) 'Peer victimization in children with Attention Deficit Hyperactivity Disorder', *Journal of Child Health Care*, 11, 3, 248–60.

Hunt, O et al (2006) 'Self-reports of psychosocial functioning among children and young adults with cleft lip and palate', *Cleft Palate and Craniofacial Journal*, 43, 5, 598–605.

Hunt, P et al (1996) 'Creating social supportive environments for fully included students who experience multiple disabilities', *Journal of the Association for Persons with Severe Handicaps*, 21, 2, 53–71.

Hurre, T and Aro, H (1998) 'Psychosocial development among adolescents with visual impairment', *European Child and Adolescent Psychiatry*, 7, 73–8.

Ingesson, SG (2007) 'Growing up with dyslexia: Interviews with teenagers and young adults', *School Psychology International*, 28, 5, 574–91.

Johnson, HR et al (2002) 'Vulnerability to bullying: Teacher-reported conduct and emotional problems, hyperactivity, peer relationship difficulties, and prosocial behaviours in primary school children', *Educational Psychology*, 22, 5, 553–6.

Kamps, D and Tankersley, M (1996) 'Prevention of behavioral and conduct disorders: Trends and research issues', *Behavioral Disorders*, 22, 1, 41–8.

Kaplan, SG and Cornell, DG (2005) 'Threats of violence by students in special education', *Behavioral Disorders*, 31, 1, 107–19.

Kauffman, JM (1999) 'How we prevent the prevention of emotional and behavioral disorders', *Exceptional Children*, 65, 448–68.

Kaukiainen, A et al (2002) 'Learning difficulties, social intelligence, and self-concept: Connections to bully-victim problems', *Scandinavian Journal of Psychology*, 43, 3, 269–78.

Kavale, KA and Forness, SR (1996) 'Social skills deficits and learning disabilities: A meta-analysis', *Journal of Learning Disabilities*, 29, 3, 226–37.

Khemka, I et al (2009) 'Impact of coercive tactics on the decision-making of adolescents with intellectual disabilities', *Journal of Intellectual Disability Research*, 53, 4, 353–62.

King, G et al (1997) 'Social skills training for withdrawn, unpopular children with physical disabilities: A preliminary evaluation', *Rehabilitation Psychology*, 42, 47–60.

Knox, E and Conti-Ramsden, G (2003) 'Bullying risks of 11-year-old children with specific language impairment (SLI): Does school placement matter?', *International Journal of Language and Communication Disorders*, 38, 1, 1–12.

Kuhne, M and Wiener, J (2000) 'Stability of social status of children with and without learning disabilities', *Learning Disability Quarterly*, 23, 1, 64–75.

Law, GU, Sinclair, S and Fraser, N (1988) 'Children's attitudes and behavioural intentions towards a peer with symptoms of ADHD: Does the addition of a diagnostic label make a difference?' *Journal of Child Health Care*, 11, 2, 98–111.

Leff, S (1999) 'Bullied children are picked on for their vulnerability (Letter)', *British Medical Journal*, 318, 1076.

Lewis, A and Lewis, V (1988) 'Young children's attitudes, after a period of integration, towards peers with severe learning difficulties', *European Journal of Special Needs Education*, 3, 3, 161–71.

Lewis, A and Lindsay, G (eds) (2000) *Researching Children's Perspectives*. Buckingham: Open University Press.

Lewis, A, Parsons, S and Robertson, C (2007) *My School, My Family, My Life: Telling it like it is*. London/Birmingham: Disability Rights Commission/Birmingham University.

Lindsay, G (2007) 'Educational psychology and the effectiveness of inclusive education/mainstreaming', *British Journal of Educational Psychology*, 77, 1–24.

Little, L (2002) 'Middle-class mothers' perceptions of peer and sibling victimization among children with Asperger's syndrome and nonverbal learning disorders', *Issues in Comprehensive Pediatric Nursing*, 25, 1, 43–57.

Luciano, S and Savage, RS (2007) 'Bullying risk in children with learning difficulties in inclusive educational settings', *Canadian Journal of School Psychology*, 22, 1, 14–31.

Lynas, W (1986) 'Pupils' attitudes to integration', *British Journal of Special Education*, 13, 31–3.

Marini, Z, Fairbairn, L and Zuber, R (2001) 'Peer harassment in individuals with developmental disabilities: Towards the development of a multidimensional bullying identification model', *Developmental Disabilities Bulletin*, 29, 2, 170–95.

Martlew, M and Cooksey, C (1989) 'The integration of a child with cerebral palsy into a mainstream nursery', *European Journal of Special Educational Needs*, 4, 103–16.

Martlew, M and Hodson, J (1991) 'Children with mild learning difficulties in an integrated and in a special school: Comparisons of behaviour, teasing and teacher's attitudes', *British Journal of Educational Psychology*, 61, 3, 355–72.

McIntyre, D 'Researching schools', in McLaughlin, C et al (eds)(2008) *Networking Practitioner Research*. London: Routledge.

McLaughlin, C, Byers, R and Oliver, C (2011) *Responding to Bullying among Children with Special Educational Needs and/or Disabilities – Knowledge phase: Part 3 – Validating practice*. London: Anti-Bullying Alliance.

McLaughlin, C, Byers, R and Peppin-Vaughan, R (2010a) *Responding to Bullying among Children with Special Educational Needs and/or Disabilities – Knowledge phase: Part 2 – A comprehensive review of the literature*. London: Anti-Bullying Alliance.

McLaughlin, C, Byers, R and Peppin-Vaughan, R (2010b) *Responding to Bullying among Children with Special Educational Needs and/or Disabilities – Knowledge phase: Part 1 – A scoping study*. London: Anti-Bullying Alliance.

McLaughlin, C et al 'Introduction', in McLaughlin, C et al (eds)(2008) *Networking Practitioner Research*. London: Routledge.

Mencap (2007) *Don't Stick It, Stop It! Bullying Wrecks Lives: The experiences of children and young people with a learning disability*. London: Mencap.

Mishna, F (2003) 'Learning disabilities and bullying: Double jeopardy', *Journal of Learning Disabilities*, 36, 4, 336–47.

Montes, G and Halterman, JS (2007) 'Bullying among children with autism and the influence of comorbidity with ADHD: A population-based study', *Ambulatory Pediatrics*, 7, 3, 253–7.

Mooney, S and Smith, PK (1995) 'Bullying and the child who stammers', *British Journal of Special Education*, 22, 1, 24–7.

Moore, S (2009) *Children who have Experienced Bullying: Performance pointers NI69*. Dartington: Research in Practice.

Morris, J (1998) *Still Missing? Volume 2: Disabled children and the Children Act*. London: Who Cares? Trust.

Morrison, GM and Furlong, MJ (1994) 'Factors associated with the experience of school violence among general education, leadership class, opportunity class, and special class day pupils', *Education and Treatment of Children*, 17, 3, 356–70.

Murphy, T and Heyman, I (2007) 'Group work in young people with Tourette syndrome', *Child and Adolescent Mental Health*, 12, 1, 46–8.

Nabuzoka, D (2003) 'Teacher ratings and peer nominations of bullying and other behaviour of children with and without learning difficulties', *Educational Psychology*, 23, 3, 307–21.

Nabuzoka, D and Smith, PK (1993) 'Sociometric status and social-behavior of children with and without learning difficulties', *Journal of Child Psychology and Psychiatry and Allied Disciplines*, 34, 1435–48.

Nakken, H and Pijl, SJ (2002) 'Getting along with classmates in regular schools: A review of the effects of integration on the development of social relationships', *International Journal of Inclusive Education*, 6, 1, 47–61.

National Deaf Children's Society (2006) *Bullying and Deaf Children: A guide for schools*. London: National Deaf Children's Society.

Newberry, MK and Parish, TS (1987) 'Enhancement of attitudes towards handicapped children through social interactions', *Journal of Social Psychology*, 127, 59–62.

Nordmann, N (2001) 'The marginalisation of students with learning disabilities as a function of school philosophy and practice', *Journal of Moral Education*, 30, 3, 273–86.

Norwich, B (2008) 'What future for special schools and inclusion? Conceptual and professional perspectives', *British Journal of Special Education*, 35, 3, 136–43.

Norwich, B and Kelly, N (2004) 'Pupils' views on inclusion: Moderate learning difficulties and bullying in mainstream and special schools', *British Educational Research Journal*, 30, 1, 43–65.

Ofsted (Office for Standards in Education, Children's Services and Skills) (2011) *The Framework for School Inspection*. September 2011, 090019. London: Ofsted.

Olweus, D (1978) *Aggression in the Schools: Bullies and whipping boys*. Washington DC: Hemisphere.

O'Moore, AM and Hillery, B (1989) 'Bullying in Dublin schools', *The Irish Journal of Psychology*, 10, 426–41.

Pavri, S and Monda-Amaya, L (2001) 'Social support in inclusive schools: Student and teacher perspectives', *Exceptional Children*, 67, 3, 391–411.

Pepler, DJ et al (1994) 'An evaluation of an anti-bullying intervention in Toronto schools', *Canadian Journal of Community Mental Health*, 13, 95–110.

Perry, DG, Kusel, SJ and Perry, LC (1988) 'Victims of peer aggression', *Developmental Psychology*, 24, 807–14.

Peterson, JS and Ray, KE (2006) 'Bullying and the gifted: Victims, perpetrators, prevalence, and effects', *Gifted Child Quarterly*, 50, 2, 148–68.

Pope, AW, Bierman, KL and Mumma, GH (1991) 'Aggression, hyperactivity, and inattention-immaturity: Behavior dimensions associated with peer rejection in elementary school boys', *Developmental Psychology*, 27, 4, 663–71.

Porter, J and Lacey, P (2005) *Researching Learning Difficulties: A guide for practitioners*. London: Paul Chapman Publishing.

Rigby, K (2000) 'Effects of peer victimization in schools and perceived social support on adolescent well-being', *Journal of Adolescence*, 23, 57–68.

Rigby, K (2005) 'Why do some children bully at school? The contributions of negative attitudes towards victims and the perceived expectations of friends, parents and teachers', *School Psychology International*, 26, 2, 147–61.

Roberts, J (1995) 'A mother's thoughts on bullying, failure and one special needs child', *Pastoral Care in Education*, 13, 2, 23–4.

Roberts, C and Zubrick, S (1992) 'Factors influencing the social status of children with mild academic disabilities in regular classrooms', *Exceptional Children*, 59, 3, 192–202.

Roland, E and Galloway, D (2002) 'Classroom influences on bullying', *Educational Research*, 44, 3, 299–312.

Rose, CA, Espelage, DL and Monda, ALE (2009) 'Bullying and victimisation rates among students in general and special education: A comparative analysis', *Educational Psychology*, 29, 7, 761–76.

Rose, R and Howley, M (2003) 'Structured approaches to the inclusion of pupils with autistic spectrum disorder in group work'. Unpublished paper presented at the European Conference on Education Research, University of Hamburg, Germany, 17–20 September 2003.

Rourke, B (1989) *Nonverbal Learning Disabilities: The syndrome and the model*. New York: Guilford Press.

Sale, P and Carey, DM (1995) 'The sociometric status of students with disabilities in a full inclusion school', *Exceptional Children*, 62, 1, 6–19.

Salmon, G and West, A (2000) 'Physical and mental health issues related to bullying in schools,' *Current Opinion in Psychiatry*, 13, 4, 375–80.

Savage, R (2005) 'Friendship and bullying patterns in children attending a language base in a mainstream school', *Educational Psychology in Practice*, 21, 1, 23–36.

Saylor, CF and Leach, JB (2009) 'Perceived bullying and social support in students accessing special inclusion programming', *Journal of Developmental and Physical Disabilities*, 21, 69–80.

Sebba, J and Robinson, C (2010) *Evaluation of Unicef UK's Rights Respecting Schools Award Executive Summary*. UK: Unicef.

Sharp, S (1996) 'The role of peers in tackling bullying in schools', *Educational Psychology in Practice*, 11, 4, 17–22.

Singer, E (2005) 'The strategies adopted by Dutch children with dyslexia to maintain their self-esteem when teased at school', *Journal of Learning Disabilities*, 38, 5, 411–23.

Siperstein, GN and Bak, JJ (1985) 'Effects of social behaviour on children's attitudes toward their mildly and moderately retarded peers', *American Journal of Mental Deficiency*, 90, 319–27.

Siperstein, GN and Gottlieb, J (1977) 'Physical stigma and academic performance as factors affecting children's first impressions of handicapped peers', *American Journal of Mental Deficiency*, 81, 455–62.

Skär, L (2003) 'Peer and adult relationships of adolescents with disabilities', *Journal of Adolescence*, 26, 6, 635–49.

Smith, JS et al (2004) 'The effectiveness of whole-school anti-bullying programs: A synthesis of evaluation research', *School Psychology Review*, 33, 4, 547–60.

Smith, P and Sharp, S (1994) *School Bullying: Insights and perspectives*. London: Taylor and Francis.

Smith, PK (2004) 'Bullying: Recent developments', *Child and Adolescent Mental Health*, 9, 3, 98–103.

Smith, PK, Pepler, D and Rigby, K (eds) (2004) *Bullying in Schools: How successful can interventions be?* Cambridge: Cambridge University Press.

Smith, PK et al (2008) 'A content analysis of school anti-bullying policies: Progress and limitations', *Educational Psychology in Practice*, 24, 1, 1–12.

Stinson, M, Whitmire, K and Kluwin, T (1996) 'Self-perceptions of social relationships in hearing-impaired adolescents', *Journal of Educational Psychology*, 88, 132–43.

Storch, EA, Masia-Warner, C and Brassard, MR (2003) 'The relationship of peer victimization to social anxiety and loneliness in adolescence', *Child Study Journal*, 33, 1–18.

Sveinsson, AV (2006) 'School bullying and disability in Hispanic youth: Are special education students at greater risk of victimization by school bullies than non-special education students?' *Dissertation Abstracts International Section A: Humanities and Social Sciences*, 66, 9A, 3214.

Sweeting, H and West, P (2001) 'Being different: Correlates of the experience of teasing and bullying at age 11', *Research Papers in Education*, 16, 3, 225–46.

Taylor, AR, Asher, SR and Williams, GA (1987) 'The social adaptation of mainstreamed mildly retarded children', *Child Development*, 58, 1321–34.

Thompson, D, Whitney, I and Smith, PK (1994) 'Bullying of children with special needs in mainstream schools', *Support for Learning*, 9, 103–6.

Tippett, N, Houlson, C and Smith, P (2010) *Prevention and Response to Identity-based Bullying among Local Authorities in England, Scotland and Wales*. Equality and Human Rights Commission, Research Report 64. London: EHRC.

Torrance, DA (2000) 'Qualitative studies into bullying within special schools', *British Journal of Special Education*, 27, 1, 16–21.

Turnbull, J (2006) 'Promoting greater understanding in peers of children who stammer', *Emotional and Behavioural Difficulties*, 11, 4, 237–47.

Twyman, KA et al (2010) 'Bullying and ostracism experiences in children with special health care needs', *Journal of Developmental and Behavioral Pediatrics*, 31, 1, 1–8.

United Nations (1989) *Convention on the Rights of the Child* (Document A/RES/44/25). Geneva: UN General Assembly.

Unnever JD and Cornell, DG (2003) 'Bullying, self-control, and ADHD', *Journal of Interpersonal Violence*, 18, 2, 129–47.

van Roekel, E, Scholte, RHJ and Didden, R (2010) 'Bullying among adolescents with Autism Spectrum Disorders: Prevalence and perception', *Journal of Autism and Developmental Disorders*, 40, 1, 63–73.

Vetter, DK (1982) 'Language disorders and schooling', *Topics in Language Disorders*, 2, 13–19.

Warne, A (2003) 'Establishing peer mediation in a special school context', *Pastoral Care in Education*, 21, 4, 27–33.

Watts, IE and Erevelles, N (2004) 'These deadly times: Reconceptualizing school violence by using critical race theory and disability studies', *American Educational Research Journal*, 41, 2, 271–99.

Wenz-Gross, M and Siperstein, GN (1997) 'Importance of social support in the adjustment of children with learning problems', *Exceptional Children*, 63, 2, 183–93.

Whitney, I, Nabuzoka, D and Smith, PK (1992) 'Bullying in schools: Mainstream and special needs', *Support for Learning*, 7, 1, 3–7.

Whitney, I and Smith, PK (1993) 'A survey of the nature and extent of bullying in junior/middle and secondary schools', *Educational Research*, 35, 1, 3–25.

Whitney, I, Smith, PK and Thompson, D 'Bullying and children with special educational needs', in PK Smith and S Sharp (eds)(1994a) *School Bullying: Insights and perspectives*. London: Routledge.

Whitney, I, Smith, PK and Thompson, D (1994b) 'Bullying of children with special needs in mainstream schools', *Support for Learning*, 9, 3, 103–6.

Woods, S and White, E (2005) 'The association between bullying behaviour, arousal levels and behaviour problems', *Journal of Adolescence*, 28, 3, 381–95.

Yoneyama, S and Naito, A (2003) 'Problems with the paradigm: The school as a factor in understanding bullying (with special reference to Japan)', *British Journal of Sociology of Education*, 24, 3, 315–30.

Young, S (1998) 'The support group approach to bullying in schools', *Educational Psychology in Practice*, 14, 1, 329.

Yude, C and Goodman, R (1999) 'Peer problems of 9 to 11-year-old children with hemiplegia in mainstream schools. Can these be predicted?', *Developmental Medicine and Child Neurology*, 41, 1, 4–8.

Yude, C, Goodman, R and McConachie, H (1998) 'Peer problems of children with hemiplegia in mainstream primary schools', *Journal of Child Psychology and Psychiatry*, 39, 4, 533–41.

Yuen, M, Westwood, P and Wong, G (2007) 'Bullying and social adjustment in a sample of Chinese students with specific learning disability', *Special Education Perspectives*, 16, 2, 35–52.

Appendices

Introduction to appendices

The following two appendices give a review of the methodological issues pertaining to the literature review and validated practice exercise (Chapters 1, 2 and 5). In outlining details of the literature review, we present details of first, how the literature review was conducted and second, the nature of the evidence base that was assessed. The discussion of the validated practice exercise also gives a methodological account of how the examples of anti-bullying interventions were generated. Limitations of both research strands are also considered.

Appendix 1: Literature review

The literature review was conducted in response to questions set by the Anti-Bullying Alliance and raised by the DCSF/DfE:

1. What does the evidence say are the most effective responses that schools can take to a) preventing and b) responding to the bullying of children with SEN and/or disabilities?

2. What evidence is there that children and young people with SEN and/or disabilities are disproportionately vulnerable to experiencing bullying and/or peer victimisation within the school context?

3. What is particular about this group of children in respect of their vulnerability to bullying, in the context of their interactions with peers?

4. What does the evidence tell us about the challenges that schools face in effectively preventing and responding to the bullying of children with SEN and/or disabilities?

Initially, a scoping study was completed to confirm the viability of the research questions; test out the search parameters; assess the nature and scope of the evidence base available for answering these questions; and provide an initial overview of trends in the literature (see McLaughlin et al 2010b). Building on the broad range of methods employed in the scoping study, the literature review identified relevant material through:

- searching bibliographic databases (including: Applied Social Sciences Index and Abstracts (ASSIA), Australian Education Index, British Education Index, ChildData, International Bibliography of the Social Sciences, PsychArticles/PsychInfo, Social Care Online, Social Sciences Citation Index, Social Services Abstracts, Zetoc, and JSTOR)
- searching project and organisation websites
- contacting individuals working in relevant organisations
- following recommendations from the National Children's Bureau and ABA
- exploring further references gathered from the full text of relevant articles.

Three screening stages were undertaken to filter out the materials most relevant to the research questions (see the Appendix of McLaughlin et al 2010a for a full description of the criteria used at each stage).

Screening 1

This was carried out using record titles and abstracts (where available) to ensure that the search results conformed to the search parameters and were relevant for answering the scoping study questions. Materials were excluded if they:

- did not address the issue of bullying
- were published before 1990
- did not relate to a study in an English-speaking country, or were not published in English
- did not relate to the research questions
- reported on the causal effect of bullying on mental health problems and disorders
- were not as full as a report published elsewhere
- were duplicate records.

Table A1 shows the number of items found in the initial search, and selected at each screening stage, by each database searched.

Table A1: Initial search results

Database	Items found	Items selected for consideration (screening 1)
Applied Social Sciences Index and Abstracts (ASSIA)	16	6
Australian Education Index	355	25
British Education Index	190	36
ChildData	530	126
International Bibliography of the Social Sciences	96	14
PsycArticles/PsycInfo	208	32
Social Care Online	64	23
Social Sciences Citation Index	397	88
Social Services Abstracts	183	15
ZeToC	14	8
JSTOR	13	1

Records from the first stage of screening were then gathered and disseminated for the second screening.

Screening 2

Following further discussions about inclusion and exclusion criteria, materials were excluded if they:

- focused on ADHD-related 'behavioural' problems/disorders
- explored bullying that was either between adults or pre-school children
- investigated the effectiveness of medical treatments for aggressive behaviour or ADHD
- investigated aggression and bullying that was occurring in non-school contexts (e.g. at home, between parents or siblings, or carers).

After the second screening, full text versions of the articles were collected where possible and read for analysis, to assess the evidence base for each of the research questions.

Screening 3

There was some considerable discussion within the research team about which literature was to be included at this stage (see Cause and effect, below). This phase therefore included a revisiting of the literature that had been excluded in the second screening, in order to confirm the criteria applied to this study. The decision was then made to adopt a refined definition of SEN and/or disabilities: one which did not include mental health disorders; other physical differences or medical conditions; and 'gifted' children. The previously excluded literature was therefore reviewed again, alongside the included articles, as well as additional literature that had been sourced from full text articles and from further consultations with individuals.

Sources were sorted according to primary or secondary importance, or excluded entirely from the study. The quality and nature of the material was recorded on 'report cards', with summaries of the findings in relation to each research question. Certain key findings from earlier research were noted at this stage. These references were followed up and, where relevant, allusions to these sources have been included in the review.

The full list of the 278 final selected sources is provided in the References section of the original report (McLaughlin et al 2010a). The majority of them are also used in Chapter 1.

The review process was monitored through a series of meetings held with Anti-Bullying Alliance (ABA) at the National Children's Bureau; and through consultations with other interested parties and key commentators.

Limitations

The following limitations should be noted.

- In some cases, we were unable to locate full text versions of the articles selected through the screening process, because they were available only in overseas libraries.
- The review largely concerns studies published since 1990. However, few articles were found from the period preceding this and the

bulk of research is understood to have been conducted in the 1990s and beyond. We suggest that any significant research in the period immediately prior to this is likely to have been referred to in the papers we reviewed and, where relevant, the review alludes to these findings.

- Many of the individuals and organisations we contacted did not reply in time for inclusion in the review.
- The review has been a time-limited exercise, enabling the team to explore the available literature and analyse the cross-cutting characteristics of the evidence base; however it was not possible to engage in the same depth with broader literature on bullying.
- The review was limited to English-language studies only.
- The evidence base for school interventions, particularly in terms of high-quality evaluations, was limited, which in turn restricted the conclusions for Research Questions 1 and 4.

Nature of the evidence base

The majority of papers were from studies in the UK or the US; with a small proportion from other countries (including Australia, Canada, Israel, Jordan, the Netherlands, Scandinavia and Hong Kong); and some interesting comparative studies from multiple locations. The literature addressed bullying in a mixture of mainstream and special schools (sometimes with comparisons between settings). Research tended to focus on the incidence of bullying in relation to specific disabilities, with less attention to the experiences of the general population of children with SEN and/or disabilities within mainstream schools. This review therefore attempts to bring together such disparate case studies.

The review also considers different types of literature that explore these issues. These include: research articles in peer-reviewed journals; reports produced by voluntary sector organisations (such as Mencap); consciousness-raising and polemical literature from advocacy groups; policy-related literature produced by government departments; enquiries carried out by the voluntary sector; and speculative work identifying problems and hypothesising on possible responses.

Gaps in the evidence base

Some anti-bullying approaches that have been developed for use in mainstream schooling (for example, staff training, 'circle of friends', and peer mentoring) have been applied to children with SEN and/or disabilities, but there is little research so far on the effectiveness of these strategies. Also, most studies relate to particular forms of SEN or categories of disability, and there has been hardly any 'overview' work done on strategies that might cover all children with SEN and/or disabilities. Further, there is very little action research or, where this has been conducted, it has been on a small scale. In this way, the existing literature is not specifically geared to resolving the problem, although the final chapter of *Perspectives on Bullying and Difference* suggests some possible future directions that research and practice might take.

Cause and effect

The main subjects of this study, as defined by the research questions, are children with SEN and/or disabilities who are bullied. However, a significant proportion of the literature addresses the anti-social and aggressive behaviour of children with particular forms of SEN and/or disabilities (for example, those with autism, Asperger's syndrome or ADHD) towards their peers, and the challenges that schools face in reducing this. There is some discussion about whether over-aggressive behaviour should be classified in itself as a disability; but this review does not engage significantly with the literature on challenging behaviour, unless it discusses an association with bullying and/or being bullied. Further, many studies examine the significance of bullying in terms of causing mental health problems (especially anxiety and depression) (for example, Rigby 2005). This literature was also excluded from this study as it did not relate closely enough to the research questions, but these are clearly significant problems that also affect young people with SEN and/or disabilities.

Some questions also need to be raised about the ways in which the literature sets up the issue of bullying. Children with certain forms of SEN and/or disabilities are often positioned within studies as having characteristics that make them inherently likely to be bullies and/or bullied, meaning that the research avoids exploring the interactions and relationships between bullies and victims and the significance of aspects of the school context. Thus one characteristic of the evidence base is the tendency to employ a 'deficit model': labelling children as 'maladjusted', 'anti-social' or 'aggressive', or as having characteristics making them likely to be bullies or bullied in the future. Other research suggests that this view is too simplistic: some studies build on the benefits of employing a 'social model' of disability and bullying, which looks not only at the characteristics of one individual but also at the social and interpersonal environment in which the bullying occurs. This also relates to broader debates in the school violence literature over whether some forms of behaviour should be classified as 'deviance', when instead attention should be paid to the needs and conditions of individuals (for example, Watts and Erevelles 2004).

Appendix 2: Validated practice

The information on which Chapter 5 is based was drawn from a research exercise designed to gather both a snapshot and interrogation of local 'validated practice' amongst schools and other agencies that respond to bullying among children with SEN and/or disabilities. The aim of the research was to review examples of practice (including both preventative and responsive interventions) used currently in schools. It also aimed to consider views raised by practitioners in validating, among themselves, the success of these practices. Such an exercise aimed to provide more insight and understanding into the challenges that schools face in preventing and responding to the bullying of children with SEN and/or disabilities.

The central method used to gather examples of practices was a national call for evidence distributed by email to schools and related bodies. The scope was wide: contact was made with mainstream schools, special schools, independent and maintained schools and academies, as well as local authorities and voluntary organisations. Representatives were reached via regional SEN networks and with the assistance of a number of key advocates including the Anti-Bullying Alliance's SEN/D expert group; and national voluntary organisations, including Nasen, Foundation for People with Learning Disabilities, Changing Faces, British Stammering Association and Mencap. Other known contacts were exploited, including regional schools working in partnership with the Faculty of Education at Cambridge University through the PGCE programme, SUPER (Schools–University Partnership for Educational Research) and HertsCam initiatives (a network of teachers and schools working in collaboration with the Faculty of Education at Cambridge University). We also approached other experienced advisors identified as developing good practice in the literature review stage of the project.

Our initial call was supplemented by intensive email and personal telephone contact over three weeks to encourage contacts to respond. We used this time to distribute the call further, through other known hubs and mailing lists, to identify other interventions. It is unknown how many recipients the call reached because of the networked nature of its distribution, but there is evidence to suggest it was nationwide, as responses were volunteered from representatives from such diverse areas of England as Dorset, the Isle of Wight, Newcastle and Wiltshire.

In the initial contact, the purpose of the exercise was to gather a list of schools and other agencies who offered interesting examples of practice in responding to bullying and victimisation of children and young people with SEN and/or disabilities. This purpose was made explicit, emphasising that we wanted to consider whether schools are using the measures identified in the review of existing research or whether, indeed, they were developing their own responses that were not yet being written about in published sources. It was made clear that the practice did not have to be comprehensive; and that our aim was to consider both practices that have been evaluated as well as those that schools believed to be effective on the basis of skilled judgement and intuition. In particular, we asked for any of the following, that is interventions:

- focused on prevention
- reactive or responsive, that is, designed for use as problems occur
- targeted on the needs of particular groups of young people
- focused on:
  - social skills
  - language and communication
  - the development of empathy among peers
- based on training, awareness-raising or development opportunities for staff
- based on peer support
- focused on consultation with pupils
- focused on consultation with parents or carers.

Interested participants were invited to complete a short record sheet outlining their intervention (see McLaughlin et al 2011, p.37), which gave details of how many people were involved in the practice; how long they had been working in this way; background details on the school or agency; and some detail on the evaluation undertaken.

On the basis of the responses received, we invited respondents to attend an event at the University of Cambridge to validate the practice: in other words, to interrogate the interventions they brought, in an informal environment with peers working around this issue; and assess the extent to which the responses are known to be effective. Not all of the respondents to the initial call were able to attend, but 21 participants representing 18 different schools or organisations attended (an additional three participants were unable to come on the day). Participants at the seminar included five representatives from local authorities; three from voluntary organisations; three teachers at special schools; nine teachers from mainstream schools; and one representative from a research institution.

During the event, practitioners worked in small groups, preparing accounts of their practice to present to the other group members. The other group members listened to these accounts, and were encouraged to ask questions to judge to what extent the practice was validated already and consider both the strengths and weaknesses of the practice. The day ended with a plenary session, allowing practitioners to share their views on where practice and school policy should be directed, what the priorities should be, and how far this diverged from the actual state of affairs.

The final stage of the exercise involved telephone interviews with school headteachers, teachers and officials from local authorities who were identified consequently as offering further interesting practice. As was the case in the conference, interviewees were invited to discuss their practice, outline the contexts within which it was applied, and reflect on its effectiveness. The interviews were recorded. Details of participants in both stages are provided in full in McLaughlin et al (2011).

Limitations

The combined exercise generated numerous examples of practice, although the time-limited nature meant that undoubtedly there were individuals with potentially relevant experience who did not participate. We also found that in the current financial climate, it was not always possible for all local authorities offering to accommodate our requests to actually do so, as they were in the midst of a period of turbulence, uncertainty and restructuring. Ultimately, the exercise relied on the willingness of individuals to contribute and provide accounts; and there were occasions when the confidentiality restrictions in various hubs prohibited the possibility of direct contact with potential participants, who were known by trusted professionals to be able to offer interesting practice examples. The report is therefore dependent on voluntary accounts of practitioners' practice, rather than being drawn from observations or any other methods employed by the research team.

Glossary of abbreviations

ADD – attention deficit disorder
ADHD – attention deficit disorder
ASD – autism spectrum disorder
LSA – learning support assistant
OCD – obsessive-compulsive disorder
SBED – social, behavioural and emotional difficulties
SEN – special educational needs
SENCo – special educational needs co-ordinator
SpLD – specific learning difficulties
TA – teaching assistant

Index

Anti-Bullying Alliance 2
awareness-raising 32
   local authority initiatives 70–1
   peers 76–7
   public 101

bullying
   definition issue 3, 37, 92, 98
   rates 5–6
   types 7–8, 55–7
   vulnerable groups 5

carers see parent/carer perspectives
causal factors 9–18
characteristics of victims 9–10, 18–19
Children Act (1998) 39–40
children/young people's perspectives
      39–40, 52–3
   behaviours 41–4
   effects 44–5
   and future roles 98–9
   recommendations 47–52
   reporting 45–7
   research findings 93–4
communication
   language and 12–14, 19
   see also social skills
'comorbid conditions' 6–7
confidence-raising 81–2
Council for Disabled Children 40, 41
counselling 81

Department for Education and Skills
      (DfES) 1–2
detection/finding out 33–5, 58
direct and relational bullying 7–8, 26–7,
      55
Disability Discrimination Act (2005)
      40

effects on victims 14, 44–5, 57–8
   additive 7, 18, 91
environmental context interventions 73–5
Equality Act (2010) 100
Equality and Human Rights
      Commission (EHRC) 2, 12, 16, 18,
      32, 34, 35, 100
evidence-based responses 86–7
external interventions 70–3

family perspectives see parent/carer
      perspectives
Farmer, TW 24
Farrington, DP and Ttofi, MM 84
fear of retribution 45–6
finding out/detection 33–5, 58

Hargreaves, DH 39

identity-based bullying 56–7
individual empowerment interventions
      81–3, 93
interventions 21–7
   evaluation 83–4, 92–3
   messages from research 23–4, 35–8
   practitioners' use of 26–7
   typologies 69–83, 88
   see also prevention; schools/school
      practitioners

language and communication, role of
      12–14, 19
leadership 85
local authority initiatives 70–3

monitoring 71–2, 86
   detection and 33–5
   future practice agenda 99–100
Morris, J 40

negative school responses 61–2
non-punitive approaches 94
non-victimized groups 7
not being believed 46–7

Ofsted 1, 100
Olweus, D 1

parent/carer perspectives 54–5
    effects 57–8
    finding out 58
    guidance for 65–6
    recommendations 64–6
    research findings 94–5
    school responses 58–63
    types and nature of bullying 55–7
peer groups 25–6, 76–80
policy 71–2
    curriculum and ethos 97–8
    future agenda 100–1
    and strategies 85–6
positive school responses 59–60
practice, future agenda 97–100
practitioners *see* schools/school
        practitioners
prevention
    children/young people's
        perspectives 47–9
    practitioner training 70–1, 99
    small group work 77–8
    see also interventions
protective factors 16–18
public awareness campaigns 101

relational and direct bullying 7–8,
        26–7, 55
research
    findings 90–5
    future agenda 96–7
    implications 95–101
    literature review 104–8 *appendix*
    main messages 23–4, 35–8
    types of studies 21–3, 28–9
    validated practice 109–11 *appendix*
    warrants 88–9
retaliation 47

schools/school practitioners
    challenges 27–32
    context 14–16, 19–20, 68, 93
    future practice agenda 97–100
    guidance for 64–5
    recommendations 85–9
    responses to parents/carers 58–63
    role 8–9
    training 70–1, 99
    types of studies 21–3, 28–9
    whole-school approach 29–32, 75–6
    see also interventions; monitoring;
        policy; prevention; research
small group work 77–8
Smith, P 1–2
social context interventions 75–7
    effectiveness 78–80, 92–3
    peer groups 25–6, 76–80
social dynamics 91–2
social skills 10–12, 19
    training 81–2
support and counselling 81

teachers *see* schools/school practitioners

understanding *see* awareness-raising
United Nations Convention on the
        Rights of the Child (1989) 39

values, questioning 87–8
vulnerable groups 5

warrants for research 88–9
whole-school approach 29–32, 75–6

young people *see* children/young
        people's perspectives